Praise

"The narrative is less a chronicle of two distinct characters than an immersion into the space between them, where devotion and grief coexist. The recurring refrain of *You and Me* becomes both a vow and a lament, evoking the fragile permanence of love. Though the wolf attack may strike some readers as heavy-handed, the heart of the book lies not in the mechanics of its tragedy but in its honest portrayal of a relationship's textures—its fights, reconciliations, and unwavering devotion. By the final pages, what lingers is the persistence of memory and the depiction of love as both an anchor and a wound. An affecting meditation on what it means to live fully in the shadow of impermanence."
KIRKUS REVIEWS

"Reading Scott's novel took me back to so many memories of what it meant (and still means) to date and find relationship as a gay man. He writes in a way that made me feel like he was reading my mind; such was the relatability to my own feelings of different experiences. If you are looking for a deep, emotionally intense insight into a gay couple's life—the good, the bad and the surprising!—this book is for you."
MARK TEWKSBURY, CC MSM, OLYMPIC CHAMPION; *INSIDE OUT: STRAIGHT TALK FROM A GAY JOCK*

"Scott Godwin goes deep: *You and Me* probes the complexities of contemporary queer relationships in a way that is at once nuanced, tender, and bracing—demonstrating the ways that the differences between men can both bring us together, and tear us apart. A strong debut from a promising new voice."
SHAWN SYMS, *NOTHING LOOKS FAMILIAR*; REVIEWS EDITOR, *PLENITUDE*

"For a story to be successful, the writer has to be compelled and the story compelling. Scott Godwin has accomplished that golden formula superbly. Highly evocative, *You and Me* is aptly titled because, on many levels, it is all of us."
MARIE BESWICK-ARTHUR, *LISTEN FOR WATER*

YOU AND ME

Scott Godwin

Published by Ingenium Books Publishing Inc.
Toronto, Ontario, Canada M6P 1Z2
https://ingeniumbooks.com

International Standard Book Numbers (ISBNs):
Paperback: 978-1-990688-61-4
Ebook: 978-1-990688-62-1

Cover Design by Jessica Bell Design via Ingenium Books

My Love,
You may not believe in what I see amongst the stars,
but one day we'll find each other there.

Table of Contents

January 2024

TEN KILOMETRES THREE times a week. Any less and he believed that the heart disease he didn't actually suffer from would kill him.

Over two decades, his mind had convinced him that his time was coming and his heart would ultimately take him. In many ways that had been true, but that was more to do with the number of times he'd allowed it to be broken than with any physical ailment. He ate well—sweet tooth aside—and exercised sometimes obsessively. Not to the extent he once had, but the sickness in his head still, after years of battling, wouldn't allow him to stop even when he needed to. Broken bones, viruses, extreme fatigue—none of these were enough to force him to get what he really needed, which was rest. He needed sleep. His tortured mind and diagnosed anxiety disorder were largely the victims of countless sleepless nights, during which either his worries or his daydreams would hold him captive.

In the darkness of our living room, I watched him stretch. Barely a glow came through the picture window from the lamps that illuminated our front walkway. This was a practice he'd begun only recently, when he discovered that loosened muscles in his chest and back led to fewer panic attacks resulting from upper-body tension while running. Prior to this, he'd taken little to no precautions before embarking on workouts. He was reckless in many ways, and though it concerned me, these remnants of his youth had endeared me to him. He was rough around the edges, and it was one of the innumerable things that I loved about him.

He was seated on the hardwood floor folded over his extended legs with his hands firmly gripping his calves. He counted his inhales and exaggerated his exhales, sinking deeper into himself with each cycle. Sometimes while doing this, he seemed about to fall asleep on top of his own legs. I wished that he would. I would have been relieved, if not happy, to see him at rest.

I looked away and focused on my own stretch. I was quiet. I was always quiet during these 4:45 a.m. pre-run rituals, but he'd often insist that I was too quiet, regardless of time or circumstance. "You really have nothing to say about this?" was a question/accusation I'd become accustomed to hearing. It would serve as the period at the end of his unravelling over one thing or another. Sometimes I did have something to say, but mostly I didn't want to fight with him. I'd always tried to avoid it where possible. I hated seeing him upset more than I hated arguing with him.

I glanced at him again as he uncurled and slowly slid onto his back to open his chest. He was oddly quiet this morning as well, the embers of the conversation we'd had prior to my falling asleep just hours earlier no doubt still burning inside of him. Ordinarily he spent the night building the bank of thoughts he couldn't wait to share with me once the day had begun and my attention was fair game, but not today. His silence was rare, and admittedly, I enjoyed seeing him like this. It was the way I'd seen him before we first spoke to each other, in the days when we were two men in a world that still wouldn't fully allow us to disclose our interest in each other with the certainty that it was safe for us to do so.

On those mornings, I would watch him move about the gym, quiet and focused. By no means a gym rat, he was devoted to his regimen and seemed to float about the room in a space that was all his own. When, on our first date, I confessed to observing him over time, he seemed taken aback that I'd noticed him at all. His quiet confidence had broken then, and I'd seen the first evidence of fault lines. He found himself unexceptional. I had noticed him, and every time I caught myself watching him, it came with a sense of certainty—I was going to know this man. Our lives would intertwine, and he would walk with me through the years. I didn't know how nor why, but he was meant to be mine.

He pulled his thin, strong frame from the floor as though he were a rag doll, making it abundantly clear that he was tired.

"The drama," I whispered.

He turned to me and mustered a playful smile.

"I forgot what it was like just to watch you," I said. "I've missed it."

"Creep," he replied, still smiling.

He stood and turned to gaze out of the window into the darkness. The street was silent and the sky glowed pink with the promise of an impending storm. He remained in this stance a few seconds too long for me not to worry that his head was taking him somewhere it ought not go.

"Hey you," I said softly. "Okay?"

He turned and gave me a nod of assurance that his expression denied. Saying nothing, he made his way to the front door to begin his struggle with his running shoes. He never bothered to unlace them after each run. Instead, he'd drag them from each heel using his opposite toes. He prematurely destroyed shoes by doing this, but I'd given up scolding him long ago and had accepted this as part of the formula that kept him a big kid at heart. He sat on the oak bench just inside the front door, head bent and focused on his task. As much as I was enjoying his silence, remnants of our earlier conversation still remained within me as well, and I knew that too many unresolved worries had kept him awake while I slept. He was worried about us, our past and our future. He worried about us always.

"Do you want my gloves?" I asked, moving toward him and extending them in his direction.

"No, I have mine," he replied quietly, without looking up from the puzzle he'd made of his laces.

"Are you sure? Mine are warm."

"I'm good," he said, irritation creeping into his voice. "I have mine."

"Yeah, but mine are—"

"Babe." He looked up at me sternly. "I have mine."

I knew better than to poke the tired bear, but this was a habit of mine, asking him something repeatedly, as though he were going to suddenly admit I was right, but knowing damn well that would never happen.

Shoes finally sorted, he stood, positioned himself in front of me, and then surprised me by leaning in to kiss me. It was tender, and the warmth of it made me want to strip the winter running gear from our bodies and return to the security of our bed together. I considered suggesting we do just that, but the very idea of skipping a run would have tortured him.

"Thank you," he said, his nose against mine. "Honestly, mine are warm enough."

"I love you," I said, my hands on his hips, keeping him close. "We have good years ahead of us and I need you to believe that. Please?"

He opened his eyes and looked deep into me. The colour of them had fallen a darker blue, as often happened while his emotions danced upward and then plummeted again, sometimes minute to minute. He reached up and touched my cheek softly with the back of his index finger. A small smile pulled up the corners of his mouth, illustrating the daily struggle between his longing to make me happy and the turmoil that existed inside of him.

"I love you more," he replied firmly, wanting me to know he meant it. I waited for him to say more, but he patted me on the chest, signalling that it was time to get moving.

Outside, our body language and initial shudders confirmed we'd both underestimated the cold this early January morning. It had snowed several centimetres earlier in the week, which would help to brighten the darkest portions of the run. Sunrise was still hours away. Again, part of me yearned to retreat to our bed, but I wanted to prove my strength to him. He'd been voicing his fears over our fourteen-year age difference more and more, and seeing me begin to slow down terrified him. It wasn't just physical. I'd developed an uncharacteristic tendency to get caught up in my head, and as of late, it had been causing me to shut down where I would have otherwise persevered.

I'd always prided myself on being physically inexorable and emotionally impassible, but his worrying had become contagious. My years as a trained athlete kept me leagues ahead of most, but time, wear, and a bad ankle were making up the difference. The realities of our future together had become heavy, and he was struggling. I knew he still found me attractive—he reminded me of this daily. Sexually we were still strong, but his fears didn't relate to this either. The idea of time running out scared him, and he repeatedly asked me if I was truly happy in our life. I got the feeling that if I'd said no, he would have turned it upside down to salvage our remaining years together. He would have. He would have done anything for me, anything for us.

We stood at the end of our driveway doing a final stretch and taking some deep preparatory breaths. Our neighbourhood was silent, dark, and fast asleep. This quietness was something that had taken getting used to. We'd had reservations about relocating to his small hometown, both having grown up in rural Ontario communities. It was a homecoming of sorts, and throughout our years here, we'd continued to rediscover what we'd both left behind decades ago—both the good and the bad. We looked back on our years together in the city with fondness and occasional remorse, but as he often reminded me, the grass is always greener. Even so, the silence at night was sometimes deafening.

We'd created a new beginning here, yet he always felt as though we'd entered our final stage. The man standing before me now with the strength, determination, and confidence to face the challenges of this frigid and snowy run wasn't the man who lay awake next to me at night, mapping out our future while also feeling like its hostage. Over the years, I'd wished that I could show him who he really was, who we really were—convince him that he didn't need to worry. I wished that I could take him to the place in my mind where I saw him, so he'd understand why he never needed to question our life, nor my love for him. I had never loved anything so much and with so much of myself. I had never known how before him.

Just as I began to feel weighed down by the cold, my ankle, and my pessimism, he stepped in front of me. His eyes, inches from mine, scanned my face, and his expression was soft but firm, as it had been moments ago inside. I could drown in those eyes a thousand times over and still pull myself up just to let him push me under one more time.

"Okay?" he asked.

"Fine," I said, already feeling my body dispute the challenge ahead.

"Are you sure you want to do this? How's your ankle?"

"Let's go," I said, as I exhaled and tried to exude a small amount of enthusiasm. For whatever reason, I was struggling today more so than other mornings and wanted this over with. I was allowing my mind to get the better of me in the very way I'd always reminded him not to do.

Before I could take a step forward, he placed his hands on either side of my face and pressed his lips against mine. His kiss was hard. It was the way he kissed me after we experienced turmoil. It was as if he felt I needed to be reminded to whom I belonged. I kissed him back but felt distant, and my internal dialogue caused me to pull away from him more quickly than I'd meant to. He noticed this and studied me for a moment, not quite wounded but curious. He patted my shoulder, scanned my eyes one last time, and then turned to launch into his run. I came to regret this moment, and would one day long for it back. I would want every moment back despite everything this man had inflicted on me. Despite everything he was about to.

The snow began falling just minutes into the run. In a better mood, I would have acknowledged how beautiful it was, but today it served only to make me more uncomfortable and less invested than I already was. He was already a good distance ahead of me and not looking back. He'd learned to exercise patience with me on days like this as I went through the motions, but I knew it was difficult for him. My holding him back was no doubt frustrating, but he protected me from this truth and never admitted it.

He'd periodically check on me and allow me to catch up before playfully patting my backside or running his finger down my spine. This morning, he appeared to be feeling strong despite his fatigue. Knowing that this area of the route was a trigger for him, I did my best to pick up my pace and stay close. I had insisted he work through his fears, and though he hated running through the pitch black of the woods, he did so three times a week in the winter months—exposure therapy—both to please me and to prove to himself that he was strong. He was. He was stronger than he ever knew he was, and if he'd been able to harness the ferocity he possessed, he'd have been unstoppable.

We exited the grounds of the old agriculture college, the buildings dark and vacant this time of day, making our way through the back end of the property and onto the trail leading through the wooded portion of our run. As anticipated, the pink sky and the snow that had fallen days prior set a glow that permitted me to turn off my headlight. We'd twice spotted an owl at this exact time and location, about twenty metres into the trail. Knowing he'd be looking for it, I'd turned off my light in hopes it would help not to alarm the animal and increase his odds of seeing it again. He felt something for it, the way he did for all animals. The first time we'd spotted it, he stopped dead and just watched it, his eyes welling. I couldn't often meet him where his heart was. Trying to imagine what it must be like to feel things so deeply left me in awe.

There was no sign of his new friend today, and I was disappointed for him. Unfazed, he stopped scanning the trees and focused on the trail ahead, forging on with an effortless grace. He would tell me time and again that I was the pretty one, but watching him now, I'd never seen anything more beautiful.

"My god, I love you," I said, under my breath.

We were deep into the trail when I had to stop briefly to give my problem ankle a moment. The wind howled around us, cutting through the dense woodland on either side of the path, and I could only just make out the sound of the snow crunching beneath his feet as he ran ahead, unaware that I'd fallen behind. I turned my lamp back on to ensure I could track him and hopefully provide him with enough light to guide his footing, though he'd insist he didn't need it.

I resumed my run with a slight limp and attempted to quicken my pace to close the gap between us. I worried he'd panic if he looked back and couldn't find me. With the glow of my light, I could make out just enough to see that he was looking over his shoulder at me, his hair wet from the snow, his cheeks flushed, smiling playfully, encouraging me to catch him. I hated that I couldn't, and felt resentful for a moment. We belonged next to each other, and I was falling behind. He'd assure me I was wrong, but we both knew it was happening in more ways than I wanted to admit. I willed myself to push harder, attempting to silence the voice in my head telling me that he'd be better off going on without me.

The towering pines that lined the trail created a tunnel that sheltered us from both the summer sun and winter storms. It wasn't a long stretch, but it was easy to feel disconnected from everyone and everything that existed on the other side of the trees. We were on our own here. No one would be passing through for hours. At times, it was his favourite place in this town. At others, such as on these mornings, when we were isolated in the darkness, it was his nightmare.

I was locked on him and pushing forward when his head suddenly snapped to the right. Something in the woods had caught his attention, and even at this distance I could see panic seize his muscles. But this wasn't a panic attack. He slowed but stayed in motion, his gaze remaining on the trees. I hoped for his sake that he had spotted his owl, but with each step that I drew closer, I could see by the tension that now held him that it was not. Whatever he'd heard, he heard it again seconds later and it brought him to a complete stop, but he remained laser focused on the woods. Dread filled me. Our conversation the previous night raced through my head. I felt panicked and unprepared. I needed more time with him. We just needed more time, and we could make everything right.

"What is it?" I called, trying to run faster, fighting my worsening ankle and the snow beneath my feet. I was too far from him. I was too fucking far from him.

He slowly turned his head and looked at me. His skin was pale, and his expression was one both terrified and apologetic. It was as though he had foreseen the next several minutes and had failed to shield me from what was to come. He jerked his head back toward the woods and slowly stepped backward. He pivoted to face me fully, and in that moment, I knew for certain that this wasn't his anxiety nor his fear of the dark woods toying with him. Something was coming, and deep inside of me, a voice that I'd always fought to keep silent told me that I was about to be faced with something from which I couldn't hide. His mouth opened, but before he could say anything, the wind carried the sound of a low snarl followed by a series of barks.

"Run!" he screamed. His instinct was, and always had been, to protect me first.

Something emerged from the forest, and before I could make sense of it, it was on him. I knew immediately that it was a wolf, but the part of me that had always forced me to deny anything I wasn't emotionally equipped to process refused to believe it. This didn't happen to people, and therefore it wasn't happening to him now. Wolves didn't lunge from the woods and attack unassuming runners.

"You can hide from life all you want, but it's still going to be waiting for you," he'd once said to me.

We'd been warned to avoid running here during these hours, due to the wildlife and how it might respond to unidentifiable beings barrelling through the dark close to their homes. I had told him time and time again that he was ridiculous to worry. This was my fault. What was happening was my fault.

I lost my footing and fell, sprawling out across the snow. When I looked up, he was being dragged by his right arm to the edge of the trail. He made no sound that I could hear, but he was fighting, using his left arm and both legs to wildly strike at it—but with too much abandon to make enough contact. The animal shook him relentlessly.

I scrambled back to my feet and screamed his name, hoping to scare off his attacker. More than that, I needed him to hear me. I needed him to know that I was coming and that I was going to save him from this. I would save him in the way that he'd believed I always had, from danger both real and imagined.

I was almost beside him, still believing there was time, when the wolf released his arm and lunged at his throat. Horror engulfed my body. Only seconds ago, this wasn't our life. Only seconds ago, my intractable mind believed we'd be dealing with a serious injury and trauma resulting from the terror of the experience, which would be over as quickly as it had begun. We'd take the time to work our way through it together. I'd take care of him as he healed. I'd smile as I listened to him recount the details with his darkest humour to those who inquired.

Now, I saw that everything my life was built upon was about to be ripped from me in the merciless way the wolf was ripping into him. My hatred toward it was instant and immense. I made the most visceral sound I could summon as I threw myself toward their bodies.

He was no longer fighting back, but the animal didn't relent. I swung my fist, connecting with the side of its head. Rather than turn on me, as I'd expected, it released its grip on his throat and scrambled over his still body. It vanished into the trees without looking back, as though it had never been there at all—as though what it had left behind meant nothing to it.

My fight response quickly turned into something else, something fuelled by the threat of losing him. I clambered on top of him, screaming his name once again. When I stopped, the silence hollowed me. He wasn't screaming, he wasn't crying, he wasn't fighting. Blood poured from the gash in his throat and soaked his chest. His right arm was limp by his side.

I lost several seconds staring at the violence of the wounds, still not convinced that this was real. Finally, guided by desperation, I furiously wiped the blood from his face so I could see him. I couldn't find him beneath what was happening. Surely I'd wake up any moment. It wasn't possible that this was happening to us. This could not and would not happen to us.

"No, no, no." My voice shook. "You're okay, baby. I'm here."

I fumbled for my phone with one hand, but it shook too much to negotiate the zipper keeping the pocket closed. Hope drained from me when I caught the expression in his eyes, which seemed to be pleading with me. The world around us slowed, and with my free hand I gently cupped his face, my thumb resting on his cheekbone.

He watched me, and I realized that he knew it was over. I stopped digging for my phone when I felt the backs of his fingers against my cheek. My eyes met his, and for a moment I felt his love run through me like water. He wasn't going to leave me like this. He wouldn't. He'd stay with me, forever warming my life. He'd promised me that, had threatened it often.

"There's nowhere you could go that I wouldn't find you," he'd once said. A lesser man would have been scared. I had pulled off his clothes and made love to him, my eyes on his from first kiss to final thrusts.

He choked, and blood sprayed from his mouth. A whimper escaped my lips as I wiped the droplets from his face, but I held his eyes, trying to stay connected to him. The episode subsided and he was still, trying to swallow but seeming unable, and I feared that the blood had filled his throat and wouldn't recede.

I moved my hand from his face to the back of his head and lifted it an inch from the snow to protect him from the cold. His fingers travelled from my cheek to slowly explore the rest of my face. A part of me would remain right here for eternity. His eyes, his touch, his slowing breath—they'd trapped me, and I didn't care if I ever left. If we could stay like this, just like this, I would accept it and ask for nothing more.

Tears filled his eyes. "I'm sorry," he said, his voice unrecognizable. "I'm so sorry."

"My love …" I said, through my own tears.

He carried guilt with him always, even when it was unwarranted. Even now, he was worried he was hurting me when he should have been fighting for himself.

I removed my hand from his face and pulled off my glove, using my teeth. His eyes still on me, I gently tilted his head and attempted to press the glove to the wound on his throat. I couldn't allow this to be my last memory of him and so I tried, with futility, to stop the blood flow—to disguise him as the man I knew.

His eyes were the colour of ice, had lost their identity, but he wouldn't look away from me. I wanted to say something, to let him know that everything was and would be okay. I searched for the right words but found nothing that could offer him any comfort.

"Don't you fucking leave me. Don't you dare fucking leave me."

He didn't flinch. He was slipping away, and that was the one thing I'd sworn I'd never let him do. We would never let each other go, no matter what. I pressed harder on the wound and caught sight of his arm. It was almost completely severed. I screamed out into the darkness, gripping him tightly. I wanted to die with him. Any hope that had remained in me poured out to join the blood that streamed from him, carrying thirteen years of us away with it.

I looked down at him through my tears, my chest heaving. His index finger slowly slid to my mouth, as though he was trying to silence or calm me. Nothing existed but the wind, the weight of his head in my hand, and the feel of his cold fingers as I intertwined his left hand with my right hand. His lips parted, and he managed to smile the same smile that had weakened me time and again.

"You and me," he said, his voice broken and barely audible, the sound of it blowing through me like splinters of glass.

He exhaled, seeming to brace himself, and after a moment he began to hum, keeping his eyes on mine. His voice wasn't his own, but the song felt familiar though I couldn't place it. It didn't matter, but I feared it mattered to him and that there was something in these last moments together that I was missing. Bewildered, I lost myself in his gaze and heartache consumed me. I tightened my grip on his head and hand as though it could keep him with me. And then, with everything I had, I prayed to a god with whom I had no relationship.

Slowly, he fell silent. I kissed his hand and held it against my lips, my teeth clenched, doing all I could to remain recognizable to him—and to show him the strength on which he'd so often relied.

"You and me," he whispered.

I flashed back to waking to the feeling of his finger running down the length of my spine, and of drifting back to sleep under his touch, knowing that he was watching over me.

As his last breath left him, his hand fell from my face. I collapsed on top of him, shaking and moaning into his chest. I freed my hand from his and wildly scrambled for my phone in a final act of desperation. Why had I stopped trying to retrieve it? It didn't matter. Nothing mattered now, and with that realization, I surrendered. I pulled my hand from my pocket and lifted my head off his. His blood stained my face and hair. I held his eyes as he left me, and in those last seconds I searched his face for peace, wanting, if nothing else, for him to feel release from himself and all that had weighed on him so heavily for so long.

"I need you," I said. "Do you hear me? I love you and I fucking need you."

What I saw in those seconds, in those eyes that owned me, was not peace. It was a promise.

2011

MORNING AFTER MORNING I watched him move about the gym with a fluidity and a quietness that made it difficult for me to take my eyes off him. I was attracted to him, but more than that, I was intrigued. What happened inside that space in which he existed? And what would it be like to share it with him? Rarely did I see him speak to other people. He was focused and seemingly too busy in his own mind to concern himself with others. I knew nothing about him and made far too many assumptions about the person I presumed him to be and the role he'd play in my life. I simply couldn't shake the belief that he was meant to be a part of me. Though I'd never been a man who subscribed to the notion of fate, something in me just knew from the first morning I saw him that with patience and time, he would one day belong to me.

At this time, my life was structured, disciplined, and had little room for disruption or investment in other people. I was focused on my work, driven by personal goals, and dependent on no one to gain satisfaction from life. I prided myself on the rigid exterior I'd cultivated and my ability to suppress any emotion that I deemed too complicated to surrender my energy to. This had cost me relationships and robbed me of opportunities that common love afforded, but I held out for something more. Someone who would see me for who I was and wouldn't ask me to change. Arrogance had led me to believe that I could do just that—expect someone to love me and conform to my world without my considering what they might need from me.

On this particular morning, he wore red. While other queer men at the gym spent exorbitant amounts on athletic attire splashed with brand names, cut to perfection, and designed to draw attention away from what little work they were actually doing, he held my attention with no such contrivances. What he wore made little difference to how his strong, lean frame appeared to me and the way he moved it. His red shorts didn't leave me questioning where he'd bought them—they left me aroused, the way they caressed his backside as he moved across the gym. He stood out in a sea of black-clad chiselled figures, and try as I might, I couldn't resist another glance each time I caught that red out of the corner of my eye.

I was making my way to the water fountain when I noticed him moving toward me from the opposite end of the floor. I tried not to look him in the eye, as I'd done for two years now, and toyed with the lid of my water bottle. As he passed, I chanced a quick look up at him and nearly startled when I realized he was looking back at me.

"Hi," he said coolly, but with a kind smile. It wasn't the first smile I'd seen on that face, but the first one directed at me.

A storm of energy surrounded me as our eyes met, and then, just as quickly, he was gone. I hadn't said hello back, too caught off guard. We'd spent countless mornings here together, and inexplicably, he'd chosen this morning to acknowledge me. I felt a not-unpleasant shiver run through my body as I allowed the contact to penetrate me. The way he'd looked at me, the sweet smile he'd worn, the sound of his voice. That one word had nearly knocked me to the ground. I shook my head and reminded myself who I was. This wasn't me. I wasn't a schoolboy, and I wouldn't be shaken by a greeting, nor spend my day reliving it.

But that was exactly what I did. I envisioned his smile and eyes and replayed his voice in my head over and over that day until I wondered if it had happened at all. I sat in meetings, delegated work to a team, and met a colleague for lunch, all the while feeling a renewed sense of purpose and, though I hated to admit it, hope. I'd wanted him for so long, and this was the first time that I'd been given reason to believe that there was an opening, that something could now be in motion.

The following day, we both made our way through our work-outs, quiet and focused and too far apart for me to establish contact again. I watched the clock and periodically checked on him, needing to know where he was, and wanting to close the distance between us. I knew that I'd need to move to the showers soon, and he'd have a schedule of his own to keep. I scolded myself for feeling so anxious and dug down to find the resolve that sometimes existed where feeling should have. I could wait. This could wait. I would not pursue him, as there was no need. Time would dictate when and how this would come to be, and I wouldn't become a man who chased. I returned my full atten-tion to the weights in my hands and didn't allow myself to scan the gym floor for him again.

A short while later I was standing before the mirror wearing only a towel around my waist and putting the finishing touches on my not-yet-fully salt-and-pepper hair, when suddenly he appeared next to me. I managed not to freeze, my mechanisms kicking in, and carried on with my work, giving him only a brief glance. He dropped his gym bag onto the counter in front of him and began to rummage through it. Realizing after a moment that it was safe to do so, I shifted my gaze in the mirror again to watch him go about his search for whatever it was he was having trouble finding. His expression was tense. He exhaled and closed his eyes for a moment, seeming angry with himself. When he opened them again, he looked at my reflection in the mirror.

"I hate to ask this," he said, appearing slightly embarrassed and notably tired. "I forgot my paste and my hair is ... I can't spend the day looking like this."

I wanted to tell him he looked phenomenal, but just smiled, raising an eyebrow. I removed my paste from my toiletry bag and held it out to him without a word.

He looked at it and then me. "You don't mind?" he asked, looking as though he were accepting a far greater favour than simply borrowing moulding paste.

I shrugged and shook my head, desperate not to visibly fall victim to his boyish charm. "Go for it."

He nodded once and mustered a smile that was polite but not entirely warm. Either he held utter indifference toward me, or he was as fatigued as his eyes suggested.

"Thank you," he said, as he took it gently from my hand.

We didn't speak as he quickly tended to himself, and I kept my eyes on my own task. When he'd finished, he replaced the lid on the small jar. He studied it for a moment before extending his arm to return it to me.

"Thanks again," he said, with another quick smile.

I reached out to take it from him and as I did, my fingers rested on top of his. For a moment, we froze in place. He noticed my touch and looked down toward our hands, suspended together, holding the jar in midair. I was unsure if this lasted seconds or minutes, but it was he who finally broke away and returned his hand to his side. He was blushing.

"I um ..." he said. "Thank you. Again." He pointed toward the jar.

"You look great," I said, immediately embarrassed that I'd let the words slip.

His smile grew, and he looked down at his bag. "Well," he said, as he pulled it from the counter. "Couldn't hold a candle to you, though."

With that, he slung his bag over his shoulder and turned to leave. As he rounded the corner, he glanced back at me shyly with a smile that nearly brought me to my knees, leaving me there in a daydream I'd never fully wake from.

Over the next few weeks, "hello" turned into "how are you," and from there we began to have actual conversations. Most of them were surface level as I maintained my effort to remain stoic. He did most of the talking and seemed content just to have my ear. More than once he chose to use a bench next to me, and it was on those mornings that I realized how natural it felt having him beside me, listening to his chatter. It felt as though he'd been there all along, and his presence warmed me.

It was a stormy October morning when he finally decided for us both that it was time to set ourselves on course for our life together. I was once again in front of the locker-room mirror, preparing myself for work, when he appeared beside me. This had become somewhat of a ritual. His reflection would appear next to mine, he'd give himself one last look, and then he'd wish me a good day before leaving me and my aching heart to watch him go. More than once I'd caught myself uttering "Stop leaving me" under my breath.

He dropped his bag on the counter and glanced at me in the mirror. "You didn't come find me today."

I knew what he was referring to but my arrogance, which often had a mind of its own, forced me to suggest otherwise. "What's that?" I asked, without looking at him.

"You didn't take the bench next to me. I didn't see you all morning."

"I apologize," I said, without sincerity, still focused on my image in the mirror. "I wasn't feeling very conversational today."

He studied me. "Not the first time, though. You're like that some days. Sort of, I don't know, removed. Makes me feel like I've done something wrong."

I was pleased that he'd noticed my absence, but not that he'd dwelled on it to this extent. Despite my longing for him, I was a person who needed to withdraw occasionally. Involuntary devices kicked in when something inside of me told me it was time to step away. But hurting him hadn't been my intention.

I glanced at his reflection. His face showed his insecurity. "You did nothing wrong," I said lightly, looking at him long enough to show him that I meant it.

He nodded and then seemed to think for a moment before rummaging through his bag. He seemed off this morning, had a sense of unease about him. I could hear his breathing. I wondered if I should ask him if he was all right, but didn't. I wasn't an uncaring person, but it wasn't in my nature to extend that sort of helping hand. Especially if it meant immersing myself in unchartered territory.

He suddenly stopped digging through his bag and placed a hand to his chest. He was still, a look of alarm crossing his face. His breath caught, and the sound of a forced inhale escaped him. I watched as he closed his eyes for a few seconds and then exhaled in a deliberate fashion. When he opened his eyes again, he stared down at the counter, slowly allowing his hand to fall from his chest. He looked exhausted. I watched him take a few more breaths and absentmindedly massage his hands.

"Okay?" I finally asked.

He looked at me as though he'd forgotten I was there, and forced himself to quickly recover. He was nervous, and seeing him this way, boyish and awkward, endeared him to me even more. I should have been more sympathetic or concerned, but I felt nothing but drawn to him in the way that I had every moment we'd shared space. He mustered a weak smile and turned to face me.

"Yeah," he said, swallowing and taking one more deep breath. "Yeah, I'm fine."

I raised an eyebrow, unsure if I should push myself to pry or if this was really none of my concern. His hands began to move about his bag again, though it seemed unlikely that he was looking for anything in particular. Rather, he was probably trying to remind himself where he'd been before becoming disoriented. He gave his head a small shake and then stopped moving. He inhaled again, looked up at my reflection, and dropped his shoulders.

"Do you want to grab a drink sometime?" he asked, looking hopeful but doing his best to appear confident.

I was caught off guard, still wondering what had just happened to him. *This is why he was so nervous*, I thought. My heart sped, and I tried to hide the look of surprise on my face, determined to keep composed and reveal to him as little as possible.

"I just thought it might be nice to get to know you outside of here," he continued. "If that's something you'd be up for. And if not, that's okay too—"

"I'd like that," I said, with just enough enthusiasm to appear sincere. I nodded lightly to reassure him. "I'd like that very much."

He smiled, his cheeks flushing slightly. "I'm free Thursday night," he said, one eyebrow raised.

Two nights later we sat at the bar in a crowded after-work spot in the city's gay village. We were surrounded by men but aware only of each other, our stools turned so we were facing and our knees touched. I was confident. I had believed this would happen if I remained patient and now, we were here. I was happy. I was grateful. He was across from me and his body was touching mine, and if I never saw him again after this evening, I'd forever remember the feel of his knees against my thighs, his pale skin in the bar light, his sandy hair falling into his eyes every time he nervously looked down at his shoes. He would be ingrained in my memory this way always.

"So," he said, rolling a straw about in his fingers and speaking just loudly enough to be heard over the hum of the bar. "Your work takes a lot of your time, you clearly take your workouts very seriously, your body is ridiculous, and you have an impeccable wardrobe. This is all I know about you really. Oh, and the type of hair product you use." He smiled.

I sipped my drink and casually rested my elbow on the bar. "I'm sure I've told you more than that."

He thought for a moment, then shook his head. "Not really, no. You're pretty guarded. I assumed it was because we were at the gym and it isn't the ideal place for getting to know people, so I never pushed you to talk more than you do. You're sweet and you seem to enjoy a good laugh from time to time, but you're not the easiest man to reach. Sometimes when we talk, I can't actually tell if I'm bothering you or if you just have nothing to offer the conversation. Then there are the days you don't talk to me at all." He paused. "But you're here now, so I guess you don't find me a total annoyance." He raised an eyebrow as if this were a question.

I was impressed and admittedly touched by his perception. He could have dismissed me as simply quiet, but he'd given me more consideration than that. He'd thought about me, and he'd noticed me. He was treating me like a human being with a personality of my own, and he was, even in these early days, seemingly working to navigate it.

"I've been content to listen," I said, trying to smile reassuringly. "You offer more of yourself than I can at this stage, but no, you're not an annoyance, not by any stretch. I find you very interesting, and I've enjoyed learning about you so far."

He regarded me, chewing on his lower lip and slowly nodding. "I'm like a documentary."

I laughed and tried again. "You are very open, and I don't mind it. I just take these things a little more slowly. I'm not a talker by nature."

He nodded again, in a way that told me he felt that was fair enough. He smiled and looked me up and down. "I guess the other boys on your dance card aren't in it for the conversation, huh?"

"My dance card?"

"Yeah." He laughed. "What? I guess your small town and my small town don't share a dialect?"

"Appears not," I said, grinning. "What is this dance card you speak of?"

His smile faded just slightly, and I watched his mind go to work behind the crease in his brow. He took his time before responding. "It's not my business, at all. I just assume, you looking the way you do, there are plenty of other guys letting you know they're free for a drink on Thursdays. And they probably talk less and fuck more, yeah?"

The sip I'd taken of my cocktail nearly escaped my mouth. I swallowed, coughed, and wiped my mouth before looking him in the eye.

"Sorry," he said. "Dance cards and foul mouths—two things we don't have in common, apparently."

I grabbed a napkin from the bar and wiped the corners of my mouth again. "It's okay," I said, clearing my throat. "You've been chatty, but shy in your way. I just wasn't expecting it, but it's okay."

"I'm nervous," he said, looking down at his shoes again. "I'm sorry. I shouldn't have said that. You're a gentleman and that was rude. I'm being rude."

I shook my head. "No need," I said. "You should just be yourself. My quietness shouldn't suggest to you that I'm delicate. I'm not offended." I patted him supportively on the thigh as though I were coaching him.

He smiled but looked embarrassed. I was realizing that his need to talk as much as he did quite likely often resulted in words he'd later wish he could retract. He didn't strike me as lacking confidence, yet he'd allowed himself to appear jealous, despite how little we knew of each other. I felt for him. He'd need to bounce back from this, and I hoped we could leave it behind us.

He studied my face. "It isn't just the way you look," he said, still seeming vulnerable. "You take up all the space in the room."

"I'm sorry?" I said, genuinely confused. "I don't know what you mean by that."

He inhaled. "It's just being around you. It's like if you're next to me, and we're talking, everything else just sort of ... maybe it's just the effect you have on people, or maybe ..."

He stared into my eyes as though he'd find in them the words to finish his thought. I wanted to help him. I wanted to tell him that it set me on fire to know he was having these feelings as well. I wanted to grab him and to stop wasting our time on this talk, and just find any and every means of keeping him as close to me as possible.

"You …" I began, and then words failed me, as they had him moments ago.

We stared at each other a few moments longer before he broke our gaze and looked at his shoes once more. His hair fell forward, and I reached over and gently brushed it away from his forehead. He looked up at me with surprise. In fact, he looked somewhat shaken by the gesture. He smiled and touched my hand briefly as I pulled it away. My stomach summersaulted and I felt disoriented.

"So," I said, shaking my head to clear it. "What else did this town of yours teach you all those years ago? Besides dance cards and a penchant for profanity?"

He seemed to snap back to awareness as well, and laughed lightly. His smile faded as he gave the question some thought. Something in it had caused a shift, and he grew serious.

"Well, certainly everything I ever needed to know about homophobia and how to hate myself for what I was." He allowed that to hang in the air a moment and then shrugged. "Small-town Ontario in the nineties, right?"

It hurt me to think that this being in front of me, whose presence brought me such warmth, had endured any type of assault or hatred in his life. He was a grown man, with a quiet confidence, and I sensed he could take care of himself, but I was suddenly overcome with the need to protect him. I wanted to tell him that whatever had happened to him during that time wouldn't happen again so long as I was around.

"From what little you've told me," he said, "your hometown sounds even smaller than mine. You must have had your share of it, no? Especially given the fourteen-year head start you had. What was that like? Gay kid in the farmlands, 1970s?"

The dreamlike state we'd existed in moments ago was giving way to adult conversation, and I was disappointed. I pursed my lips and slowly shook my head, thinking back to those years. "I was fortunate," I said. "Supportive family, small community. They didn't care. Well, most likely didn't notice. I carried myself a certain way ..."

He nodded. "You're very masculine. It seems to come naturally to you. You don't have to force it. I'm guessing that helped a lot."

"Likely. But I also never worried about it. If people were talking, I didn't hear it. I don't recall ever feeling afraid, but you're not wrong. Perhaps things would have been different if I'd not been who I was."

He stared at me a moment, taking this in. "I'm glad," he said. "I'm glad you had that experience. Truly."

I nodded, and we both fell quiet. This wasn't the conversation I'd expected while spending the afternoon quelling my nerves and excitement. It was important, and I wanted to know him, but it felt that we were quickly moving through the first-date laughs and trivial lines of questioning and directly into the meat of what made us who we were as people.

In my mind, I'd seen us come together without words and then simply exist alongside each other, allowing life to take shape as we moved through it together. This was work. He had things to say. He'd had experiences. He wanted to know who I was and who I'd been. He was unlike any man I'd been on a date with in recent years, all of whom had given up on conversation with me almost immediately and been satisfied just to have sex. I hadn't spoken with any of them since. He wasn't challenging me, but I was having a difficult time keeping up. I had revealed more about myself in the last hour than I had to anyone in some time, and this balancing act between dialogue and hypnotizing touches was dizzying.

"Did you have boyfriends?" he asked. "As a teenager there, was that possible?"

I told myself to keep going and give him what he needed. He wasn't looking for an evening of no substance followed by unanswered phone calls or messages. He was trying. I had to try for him. If I wanted everything from him, I had to prepare myself to earn it. I believed he was worth this.

"I suppose I felt free to explore?" I offered. "I didn't seek out relationships, but I knew what I wanted and where to find it. I had positive experiences for the most part."

He had a look of resentment about him that I could tell he was attempting to mask. Our formative years had clearly differed a great deal. Would this create a rift between us? If he felt that life hadn't taught us the same lessons, perhaps he'd worry that we wouldn't understand each nother. I wanted to return to the realm we'd shared moments ago, when I'd touched him.

"That's one thing I was always envious of," he said. "Anyone who got to experience first loves the proper way. Like, what must it have been like to go through all those experiences and make those memories with someone who really made you feel it. It makes me angry, y'know? Seeing it in movies but never having had it and knowing you can never go back and do it again. First kiss, first time having sex and it really meaning something— or at least enjoying it ..." He trailed off and seemed to begin burying himself in heartache. Just as quickly, he regained his composure and shrugged once again. "Boo-hoo, I know. People have endured worse."

"I wouldn't say my experiences had much to do with love," I said, hoping to downplay our differences. "I was fortunate, though. I was able to leave town and meet other men my age on weekends. I was a good boy with bad friends. They took me to where I needed to be."

He smiled at me, and I could tell this pleased him. I knew how I appeared to people, and felt proud that he found enjoyment in learning I'd once been able to act on impulse. I wanted him to see my potential and not surmise that there was little to me, the way others before him had so quickly done.

"I tried, with girls," he said. "I tried to find something real in those experiences, but that was mostly just survival, I guess."

"How so?"

He took a sip of his drink before responding. "Make people less inclined to want to kick my ass if I could pass as straight. I didn't, but I gave them just enough to leave room for doubt. Having a girlfriend, whether I liked it or not, offered a bit of protection."

I narrowed my eyes. "That really does sound terrible. To have to have forced yourself to do that."

"I was okay." He shrugged, a sly smile returning to his face. "I was a genius when it came to manipulating straight guys into believing they wanted me to blow them, so those years weren't a total loss."

I stared blankly at him, waiting for the cue that he'd been joking. It didn't come. This quiet, graceful creature I'd observed all this time was now wreaking havoc on my fantasy, and I wanted to scream and ask him what he was doing to me. I was becoming angry and frustrated, but more so, I couldn't wait to see what he'd say next. I was smitten.

"It wasn't all bad," he continued, his expression letting me know he was returning to a more civilized place in conversation, and I found myself smiling. "People say it and I believe it—growing up in a small town builds character. I can appreciate it more now than I could then. It's not the same place it was, or maybe I'm not the same person I was."

I nodded slowly. "That may be so, but it doesn't make it any less painful for you." I'd meant to stop there, but for some reason, more came. "I wish I'd been there with you."

This seemed to startle him as much as it did me. He looked at me but said nothing, cocking his head to one side and keeping his eyes on mine. I opened my mouth with every intention of retracting my statement, but the appropriate words didn't come. And deep down, I knew that I didn't want them to. I didn't know where this side of me was emerging from, but what I'd said had been true. I wished that we'd lived those years together and that I'd shared with him each and every one of those moments.

"So there's actually a big old heart in there," he said finally, gently poking my chest with his index finger, then letting it slide down my abdomen before retreating.

I smiled, embarrassed, and looked away. "I never claimed there wasn't."

He lightly kicked my shin to bring my attention back to him. "You should be careful with that tough exterior of yours. You might be denying a part of yourself something it maybe needs, yeah? Your heart can't survive on structure and discipline."

It hurt, being seen this way. I would never admit to it, but him believing that I would stifle love or notions of romance gave rise to insecurities I had buried long ago. He was exhausting me, and part of me wanted to ask him to stop speaking—but the other part of me was flattered. It was flattering to be so seen by him, and the more he carried me through this night, the more I wanted.

"So, one thing we do have in common," he said, sensing the silence was beginning to stretch. "Greener pastures." He took his glass and raised it. I obliged and clinked my glass against his. "We left home in search of a better life, and both ended up here and now."

We felt like a team in that moment, a sense of common ground—understood by most queer men of a certain age—finally established between us. None of this was what I had expected, but being near him made me feel I was something more than I was used to being. I couldn't remember the last time anyone had shown interest in who I was or where I came from. As uncomfortable as he was making me, he had me entranced.

I placed my hand on his thigh and decided to let myself go for just a moment. "I'm glad that life led you to right here, right now."

He looked down at my hand, and the room around us dissolved. The people, the music, the lights, everything seemed to slow, and I felt something course through us both, running from his leg through my arm and into my chest. We looked up at each other, the conversation vanishing and leaving behind only this. He moved his hand and rested it on top of mine, looking as though he wanted to speak but making no sound.

"I've noticed you every morning for two years now," I said, looking directly into his eyes.

He climbed slowly off his barstool then, stood between my legs and, without a word, leaned in to kiss me. Our lips connected but I felt him everywhere, and as the seconds passed, I lost all awareness and sunk deep into a place where dream and reality blurred. As he pulled away, I realized I'd taken hold of his arms and he was unable to move. He smiled, and the last recognizable part of myself abandoned me.

"Why does touching you feel like that?" he asked, looking as though he'd just woken up from a long sleep.

Before I could respond, he leaned in and kissed me once more, his left palm and fingers against my face. This time when he tried to pull away, I gently grabbed the collar of his shirt, clenched it in my fist, and pulled his face back down toward me. We paid our tab, hailed a cab, and went to his house.

We made love. It was raw, it was core-shaking, and we nearly devoured each other. I should have waited. He was sure, and my need to be as close to him as possible obliterated my intent to take this slowly. Our bodies felt at ease together, and I could have stayed that way for hours. He would pause periodically, making a point to grab my chin, look into my eyes, and kiss me. When we both climaxed, he grabbed the back of my head and held our foreheads together, sending a chill down my spine that nearly caused me to lose consciousness. I had never felt anything like the sensation of my naked body against his, and it stoned me. Making love to him brought me out of myself in a way that I'd never experienced, and when he was finished with me, I remained in that space with him.

Over the years to come, we'd disagree annually over when we became an official couple. He would half-jokingly insist that my body made a commitment to him that night, and he wasn't wrong. I felt a deal had been signed and he'd own me forever. I knew I was in love that night.

January 2024

I sat on the edge of our bed, the room dark and cold, my bare feet resting on the hardwood floor. In my lap I cradled a photo of us taken several years prior, on the balcony of our condo in the city. We were dressed for a night out during the holiday season. City lights blazed in the background, and the two of us were locked in a kiss interrupted by our smiles. If I could have managed to smile now, I would have at the memory of us then. In this photo, we appeared to be as happy as we'd truly been sometimes.

Those years had been our hardest, though. He had struggled; we had struggled. I knew that he looked back on them with some harboured resentment and lingering scars, but to me, that time was part of our journey, and I wouldn't have traded it. We differed in that way, as we did in countless others. Where I saw love and memories of the road we'd travelled, he recalled sadness, and even felt remorse. He'd be the first to admit that our life together was a beautiful one, but with a realism that wouldn't permit me to forget the worst of those times.

I caressed our faces with my fingers, the glass of the frame cold to the touch. I could feel the smoothness of his skin, the contours of his cheekbones, and if I tried, I could almost pick up the scent of the cream he applied to his face each night before crawling into bed with me. It had reminded me of orange and spice, and as I leaned in to kiss him good night, I'd take a subtle inhale, running my nose across his cheek.

I glanced up at one of the bedroom windows to the left of me. It overlooked our backyard, our small shed, two of our gardens, and the neighbourhood beyond. In the warmer months we'd both feel the romance of the breeze that would blow through these windows and encircle the bedroom, causing the curtains to sway just slightly, creating a dreamlike effect. On a clear night the stars were visible from where we lay, and this was one thing that he'd adored about this place. Some evenings, we'd listen to the wind in our trees, or the rain hitting the shed roof, feeling at ease, feeling settled.

A sharp pain hit me deep in my stomach and travelled up to my chest, forcing me to look away. Every night before coming to bed, he'd stop at that window. He'd stand silently, his fingers resting on the narrow ledge as he stared out into night. He'd stay that way for minutes on end. Sometimes I fell asleep before he finally made his way to the bed. I never asked him why he did this, or what he was looking at—or for. I simply watched as he performed his nightly surveillance, understanding that wherever his mind was in those minutes, it was an important time to him. I could see him in my memory now, clear as day, standing at his window with his face illuminated by the moon.

I took a long and slow inhale, held my breath for a couple of seconds, and then slowly released it. In the two weeks since I'd lost him, these stomach pains had become a regular occurrence, as had my habit of forgetting to breathe. I'd be lost in thought, and then suddenly find myself gasping for air and placing a hand to my gut, nearly doubling over from the sudden onset of pain. This didn't frighten me. I welcomed the suffering and believed that I deserved it. Existing without him should feel like nothing less than this.

Forcing myself not to look back toward his window, I returned my gaze to the photograph in my lap. As I did, his blood-soaked face sliced through my memory, and I shuddered violently. A whimper escaped as a wave of nausea swept over me, and I placed one hand on the bed to stabilize myself. This was also something that happened regularly now. I made a conscious effort to hold onto only the images of him that brought me warmth, but every single day, more than once, I'd be thrown back into those woods and feel it so completely that it was as though I were there, watching him die over and over again. I'd been unable to cry since that morning, but these episodes would cause a lump to rise in my throat and my body would slump as though I'd sobbed for hours.

I looked down at the photo once more and touched his face. I needed to move from the bedroom. I didn't know where to go, but I bargained with myself that if I made it to the hallway, I could devise a plan from there. I stood slowly and glanced around the room. Everything was as he'd left it, his clothes still in their drawers and his jewellery, which he never wore, in its box. All waiting for his return. My eyes watered slightly, and I hung my head, making my way out of the room.

In the hallway, I realized I was still holding the frame. I looked down at it once more and decided that I'd keep it next to me in our bed tonight when I tried, with futility, to sleep. I tossed it onto the bed, underestimating my force. The frame bounced lightly on the mattress, and I watched as it fell and landed on the cold, hard floor, face down.

The glass shattered into an alarming number of pieces. I heard us crack and then watched as we scattered in shards across the floor, our memory reduced to carnage before my eyes. I froze in place, staring down at the glass, which glinted in the winter moonlight streaming through his window. I immediately sensed that I'd harmed him, and felt sickened again. If he could see what I'd just done, he'd be hurt. I hated myself in this moment. I hated everything and wished that I could just fucking die.

I knelt, but rather than pick up the pieces, I leaned back against his nightstand and slowly lowered myself to a seated position on the floor. The photo lay between my sprawled legs. I couldn't bring myself to turn over the frame and see what remained of us.

I stayed this way for what felt like hours. I needed him. I needed him to reassure me and tell me that it was okay and then smile at me in the way he always had when he knew that my heart wasn't at ease. I needed him to forgive me for this. I felt a dizziness come over me and shivered from the cold of the room. Staring at the broken glass, I envisioned him curling into me between my legs, kissing my neck. I envisioned wrapping my arms and legs around his body to pull him close. As I sat there, imagining his body against mine, I felt the sensation of a warm and gentle weight on my shoulder.

2012

We were making our way to a downtown yoga studio on a grey afternoon. He'd suggested we meet at the front door, but knowing the route he'd take, I'd planned accordingly so that I'd find him en route.

"I told you I'd meet you there," he said, sounding slightly annoyed.

"I know, but I wanted to walk with you." I ran my hand down his back. "This way I get more time with you."

"We're spending the day together. That wasn't enough time for you?"

He was smiling to show that he wasn't intending to hurt my feelings, but I never understood why this bothered him so. If I knew where he was getting his groceries, I'd plan my day so that I could meet him there and shop with him. If he had reason to adjust his gym schedule one day, I did the same to ensure we'd be there together. And if we were planning to meet, I saw no reason for us not to make the trek to the location together. He enjoyed walking the city streets alone, but I couldn't stand the idea of idly waiting for him when I could just be with him instead.

"A week ago, I couldn't track you down, again, yet here you are doing exactly that to me," he said. "Does that seem fair?"

I tensed at the idea of revisiting this conversation. He was constantly confused about what he called my mixed messaging, and I knew he was tiring of it. I also knew that when we were together, everything was as it should be, so I paid little mind to the disturbances we experienced while apart.

"Anyway." He sighed, taking my hand in his. "Listen," he said, as we approached the studio, "you have to take this seriously."

"Relax," I said, nudging him with my elbow. I'd already found myself telling him to do that often. In our short time together, I'd come to learn that he was a worrier. There was something to concern himself with at all times.

"I can't relax if I know you're going to act like a jackass."

"I'm looking forward to this," I said with a smile. "It's new to me, and I appreciate you setting it up for us."

He glanced at me, and his eyes said *bullshit*. Spring was struggling, and we were equally stumbling our way through the springtime of our relationship. The holidays had interrupted our start, both of us having family and social obligations. Following that, I'd spent several weeks travelling for work, and though we'd kept in touch during that time, we hadn't had the opportunity to truly tend to us. Real life had intervened to remind us that it didn't care about the state of lovesickness in which we'd found ourselves after our first date.

In late January we'd met up for the first time in the new year and had been on several dates since, all with varying results. I quickly learned that he was a person who felt things deeply, and just as quickly he confirmed—as he'd already suspected—that I was not. I marvelled at how this person who'd been such a mystery to me was a fountain of compassion with more words than he knew what to do with. It hadn't been just nerves; he seemed content to talk at me endlessly, and I adored it. I'd just watch and listen as he revealed himself to me more with every conversation. He rarely pushed me to keep up. Since our first date, he'd learned to pull back and allow me to fill in the blanks in my own time. He showed me patience.

He seemed somewhat uncomfortable with certain aspects of my life, but I didn't concern myself much with the details of his. My only interest was him. The people and things surrounding him were of no consequence to me. My absences for work or unanswered calls from him ignited a telling response. He had insecurities and he had wounds, and though I wanted nothing more than to be near him, I was quick to take time to myself when I needed it. I'd always been this way, and I'd hurt others before him by forcibly taking this space. His heart had been dragged through the dirt by more than one love, and he sensed that I was capable of doing the same. He wasn't wrong. Though I remained certain that he was to be a fixture in my life, I was what I was, and I could be unintentionally cruel—I knew this. The challenge I faced was countering it by showing enough of my own heart to prove that I wasn't hopeless, that I was in this, and that he was hugely important to me. I needed to convince him that who I was had nothing to do with who I believed we would be, and that I was capable of trying.

On a recent outing, we'd visited a games bar and spent the evening drinking beer and failing miserably at each nonsport. At one point, he'd looked at me with a truly contented expression and told me that he hadn't realized how much fun I could be. He hadn't worked to bring my guard down—it just happened sometimes when I was with him. I loved being with him: He made me laugh, and I was unashamed to show that I was happy and to buck what was believed to be my norm for him. But it was a process.

"It's partner yoga," he said, as he opened the studio door for me. "That means teamwork."

I smiled again, passing by him to enter. "Yes, I get the concept."

"It isn't a race, and it isn't a competition," he continued, as we made our way up the stairs, his hand pressing against my lower back. "You aren't here to outperform anyone so just … take it easy, okay?"

I stopped on the landing and when he caught up, I grabbed his arm just firmly enough to keep him close for a moment. His observations of me in these few short weeks had been astute, and it both flattered and unnerved me. At the gym I'd attempted to push him a little harder, as I knew he had it in him, and one morning when he'd been irritable, he'd told me he didn't need my shit and walked away. He hadn't spoken to me for the remainder of his workout. It had made me laugh but I knew where he was coming from. My competitive edge knew few limits, and I knew he had that quality, though to a lesser extent. I'd watch him run to the point of exhaustion and then keep going. He did this to himself daily. We weren't complete opposites in every sense. In many ways we, in fact, seemed perfectly matched.

I leaned in and kissed him softly. "I can be gentle, you know."

He pulled away and squinted at me. "We'll see about that, cowboy."

I grinned, enjoying that he saw me this way. He'd told me one evening while play-fighting on his couch that I was a "stupid oaf of a kid." He brought it out in me. He allowed me to be so many things that I'd always kept stifled. I might not yet have struck the balance between the person I was and the person I was becoming, but he was seeing me through it.

We walked to the front desk and the instructor handed us forms. We took a seat on a bench, and he pointed out where I needed to sign.

"Thank you for being a good sport about this," he said quietly. "I know this isn't really your thing, but I just thought that maybe doing it together would be—"

I kissed him to stop his mind before it began racing. "It's a really great idea," I said, as I pulled away. "I want to be here with you."

He smiled only slightly, still unconvinced, and then focused on his form. He put the pen to his mouth while reading the fine print, which I knew he was doing for both of us. I'd signed mine without a second thought, so he was ensuring that there was nothing in the release that would place me in any kind of jeopardy. It was just yoga, but seeing him go through these motions made him all the more attractive to me. His emotions seemed chaotic at times, but when he was truly focused on something, it undoubtably involved someone he cared about. Satisfied that he hadn't placed us in danger, he winked at me and told me he'd allow me to partake. I laughed, kissed him on the cheek, and thanked him.

Thirty minutes later I was on my back with him balanced in a plank on my upward-reaching hands and feet. I took pride in how we probably looked to the others in the class and how naturally we'd both taken to this. We complemented each other well—our bodies worked together with minimal communication. His hair gently fell forward, framing his cheekbones, and his oceanic eyes held mine beneath him.

"I've got you," I whispered, my arms and legs steady.

He inhaled slowly and cocked his head, so casually it seemed he could remain there for hours. I could tell he was silently dissecting my three words. We inhaled, we exhaled, and we stared into each other's eyes, unblinking. When instructed, I slowly bent my knees and elbows to gently lower him toward me. He was supposed to dismount but remained moments longer than the other pairs had, still looking into my eyes. The others had noticed, and butterflies rose in my stomach. I was worried I might melt into a puddle beneath him. I stifled a short, nervous laugh, unsure what he was doing. He blew a soft kiss down at me and caressed my hand with his thumbs while still hovering over me, trusting me to hold him there.

"Nah," he said. "I've got you."

He extended his neck, lowered his face, and kissed me. He then carefully climbed off my hands and feet and slid onto his mat beside me. It had taken him only a moment to disarm me. I stared up at where he'd just been. He was now lying next to me on his stomach with his cheek on the floor and his face turned to me. We'd fallen out of sync with the rest of the group, and though this made me a bit uneasy, I stayed with him and tried not to worry about the eyes on us, turning my head to face him as well. He reached out a hand and slowly ran a finger across my cheek. I swallowed, feeling the same disorientation I had the day we first touched, months earlier.

The second we were done here I was going to take him home and make love to him. I wasn't even sure I could wait that long.

Seemingly reading my mind, he smiled and whispered, "Let's go."

We pulled ourselves off the floor, and he casually tossed an apology toward the instructor and the other class members. We didn't change, just left the studio and laughed as we escaped into the cool March weather, stopping on the street just long enough for me to kiss him long and hard.

A short time later he was on top of me in his bed, sweat running down his chest and abdomen and landing on mine. I grasped his hips as he rocked back and forth, nothing but our breath filling the room. I would never get enough. No day would come when I wouldn't ache to be as close to him as I was right now. I moved my hands to his face and pulled him down for a kiss, lifting my head to meet him partway. He released himself from the kiss and gently bit my lower lip. When he did this, there was always a small part of me that felt nervous. I knew he didn't want to hurt me, but something left me wondering how far he'd go.

He stopped moving and looked into my eyes. I smiled and leaned up to kiss him again, but he gently pushed me back down. I was certain that his head was full of words, but he spoke none. He leaned down to kiss me on his own terms, and it was soft. It was new. And in that moment, I was reminded that so were we. We were growing and we were learning, and it was sometimes difficult, but being connected to him this way was all that mattered to me. This was everything.

January 2024

I STOOD IN our basement and absentmindedly flipped through his CD collection. The fourteen years between us had left few gaps, as we were both young at heart, but music and movies were areas where we'd often educated each other. I recognized most of the artists, but some were more obscure—especially the ones he'd carried with him from his teenage years in the nineties. More than once, he'd lamented that we hadn't had those formative years together. He held a romantic ideal of how it would have been to share all those firsts, but we both knew that if we'd met any sooner than we had, neither of us would have been ready. We'd barely made it through each other as it was. I didn't disagree with him, though; age and stage of life had cost us opportunities that couples who'd committed in their twenties had been able to explore.

I was both relieved and disappointed that few of the album names reminded me of him. I pulled down a case that was unfamiliar to me and ambled to the stereo. The player swallowed the disc, and I hit play, then stared down at the machine, waiting to hear something, anything that would bring him closer to me. The music began and, with a bottle of wine tucked under my arm, I made my way to the couch and dropped myself onto it. I had refrained from alcohol until now for fear of what it would do to me. I was a void who barely slept, rarely ate, and avoided all contact. The only thread keeping me together was the same one that kept my emotions tied down, and I'd been striving to keep it taut. Tonight, I would surrender. I'd decided to open a bottle that he'd been saving, in an attempt to drown in it. I saw no sense in protecting myself anymore.

I emptied half of the bottle into my glass and took a long sip. I stared at the bookshelf that held only his favourites along with the music and movies that had shaped him. We had bought this house in a hurry, and he'd never entirely warmed to it, but he'd found himself at home in the basement. We'd turned it into a grown-up rec room of sorts with only the two of us in mind. We'd spent every evening down here, glued to each other on this couch, despite the abundance of space. We watched the movies we loved over and over, each one assigned to a season or holiday. We also burned through bad television, laughed at the same lowbrow humour, and encouraged each other to voice scathing reviews of anything we felt to be unworthy of our time. My favourite nights, though, were the ones when he'd put on a show that he knew only I would enjoy. On these nights, he'd lay his head in my lap and drift off as I played with his hair. It was the most peaceful he ever looked, and he'd stay that way until I woke him for bed.

Every bone in my body ached as the memories washed over me. I wanted my best friend back. I wanted to feel the weight of him pushing me into the arm of the couch as he curled up so tightly against me that trying to get an inch to myself was futile. This room had felt like home, had been warm with him in it. Now it was another vacant space occupied only by the terror that accompanied this level of loneliness. Still, being here made me feel close to him, and I'd take what little of that I could get.

The music endured, and its melancholy put me exactly where I wanted to be. He hadn't played this album for me, and I lost myself in it, letting the apparent darkness of his earlier years find its way through me via the song. He had been many things: a big kid, a solemn prince, a caregiver, a destroyer, a fighter, and a fierce lover with a heart bigger than any I'd known. Those who had assumed to know him were happy with his often-simple exterior, but listening to this, I felt him for what he was—haunting and at times impossible.

I swallowed my wine and let it stone me, sinking to a new low with each sip. I closed my eyes and wished so desperately to feel him next to me that I found myself having forgotten to breathe again. I placed my glass on the coffee table, inhaled, and then let my head hang over the back of the couch. I was angry and ashamed that I'd allowed myself to once again believe for a moment that it was possible. Feeling him near me would be a fabrication. Worse, it was the most I could hope for. I opened my eyes, hoping to see him smiling down at me before leaning in for a kiss, but a wave of dizziness swept over me and before I could fight it, I passed out.

I woke up hours later stiff and still drunk, and caught myself about to tell him that it was time for bed. I hung my head and let that kill me for a moment, then slowly stood and carried myself up the stairs. I dreaded this time more than any. I hated entering our room each night. I could have slept on the couch, but our bed remained the place I felt him the most—and I needed that more than anything right now. I had washed the sheets reluctantly, but I could still pick up the scent of him every time I pitifully crawled under the covers. His basket of unwashed laundry sat in the corner of the room. I knew it would need to be dealt with, but I couldn't yet move or remove one thing that gave me any sense of him. I needed as much of him intact as I could salvage.

I dragged myself up the four steps of our split-level toward the bedroom, feeling as though bricks were attached to both ankles. As I turned to enter the doorway, a gust of cold air hit me. It was enough to nearly render me sober. Standing still, I looked toward his window. I must have opened it and accidentally left it ajar. But surely I hadn't? I hadn't been able to bring myself to look out of it since I lost him.

I scanned the room with bleary eyes and wrapped my arms around my shoulders. Shivering, I caught myself suddenly checking the hallway behind me, expecting to see someone. I waited several moments, but whatever I was expecting to see didn't materialize, and I shook my head before stumbling toward the bed. Climbing under the covers, I shivered again, sure that the temperature in the room was continuing to drop. I felt a sense of unease as I lay there, cold and alone but also sensing that maybe I wasn't.

"Yes you are," I whispered, scolding myself for being so pathetic.

I turned onto my side, buried myself under the blankets, and wished that I could cry. I hadn't since I collapsed on top of his almost-lifeless body in the woods. I spent the darkest hours of the night this way, shivering and hoping for sleep, for refuge that refused to come. I lay awake until sunrise, willing him to climb into the bed, wrap his arm around me, and pull me close.

2012

It was late summer, and we sat next to each other on his front steps. His street was quiet aside from the occasional voices of those having exited the streetcar at the nearby stop. We both thrived in a big city but also shared an appreciation for a quiet space, for the large oaks that lined his street and the sound of birds on a summer afternoon. At our cores, we carried romance buried by life experiences.

A breeze tousled his hair as he leaned his head against the railing of the four cement stairs that led to his townhouse. He hadn't slept the night before. Near midnight I'd woken to the sound of him struggling for air. I'd tried to calm him, but he was in a state so desperate that he couldn't see his way out of it. At one point he'd grabbed my arm and gasped, "My heart," believing that it was failing him, a look of pure terror in his eyes. I didn't know anxiety and couldn't understand what he was going through. All I could do was stay with him, reassuring him until it passed, though I was certain he'd remained awake long after I believed he'd calmed. I had witnessed two or three of these attacks now, and they left him exhausted—but not enough to eradicate the fear that lingered in him.

I brushed the hair from his eyes and rested my hand on his shoulder. He stared straight ahead and seemed calm. I knew it was an illusion. A storm still raged inside of him. Any relief he felt now would have come from the sedative he'd surrendered to taking hours earlier.

"How are you feeling?" I asked.

He glanced at me as though he'd forgotten I was there.

"Fine," he replied. "I'm fine. I'm sorry."

I massaged his shoulder and inched myself closer to him. As our bodies connected, I felt his shoulder relax under my grip. He leaned into me.

"Please don't apologize," I said. "I'm so sorry that this is something you have to go through."

"I know what you must think of me," he said, not meeting my eye. "I know how weak I must look to you."

"No," I said, and meant it. "You might be one of the strongest people I know. I find it remarkable that you carry this and still manage to live your life so fully. This thing that happens to you, it isn't who you are."

He had a look of defeat about him.

"But it is," he said. "It dictates everything. Which street I should or shouldn't walk down, what time of day I grocery shop to avoid standing in a line for too long, where and when I run because I'm sure I'll die and no one will find me if I don't time it so that people will cross my path soon enough to—"

"Stop it," I said sternly. "You're not helping yourself by spinning your wheels this way. You're fine."

He closed his eyes in a clear attempt to remain patient. "It's not fine," he said calmly. "I tried medicating it but never saw it through. I hated taking that shit." After a few moments of silence, he opened his eyes. They'd taken on the colour of the August sky, but they were tired. In fact, he looked as though he were barely surviving. "It went away for a while, my anxiety. I hadn't had a panic attack in probably two years. This is the third time in a month."

I let my hand fall from his shoulder to rest behind him on the cement.

"Is it me?" I asked, looking toward the street.

He said nothing, and that silence said everything. I could feel him staring at me.

"I know how hard this has been," I said, turning to face him again. "I know that sometimes I need space and that when I do, I tend to shut you out, and that isn't always fair. If you could just understand how much I want you, if you could believe me when I tell you, then you wouldn't worry so much when we're apart. I adore you, but sometimes it's best for me to remove myself. I don't know why that is, but it is something I know about myself, so you have to trust me when I tell you that it's better for me to do it than it would be for me to be near you during those times."

"You don't need to push me away to take space, and you don't need to hurt me to prove that you still have your independence," he said, his fire returning. Though I didn't want to fight, I was relieved and proud to see him ready to. "You suffocate me at times and then without warning you just … turn it off. You shut it down, you shut your phone down, and you refuse to tell me where you are or what you're doing. Boys in college behave that way, not grown men. It sends me into an emotional spiral where I'm calling too much and leaving angry messages and hating myself for how weak I look in those moments and for how fucking small I feel. It reduces us both to being something I don't want to be, and the only reason we are where we are is because you have insisted time and time again that we belong here. You show up on my doorstep, you find me at the grocery store, you want to follow me through every mundane errand on a Sunday afternoon and it's relentless but then you just … go. You just close the door on me, and it makes everything you've said sound like a lie. We're different. We're too different, and it's been long enough now for us both to see that. We moved so fast, but it feels like we're actually just stuck in the same place. I thought we were bigger than this."

I nodded slowly. "Yes, I do that, all of it, and I'm sorry. I don't do any of those things to hurt you—you're very wrong about that. I'm sorry that I shut you out, but I'm not sorry for wanting to be with you every spare moment I have. You're right, I would find you anywhere, and I'm not going to stop doing that, whether you understand it or not. If I want to find you, I will."

He tried not to smile. "But it does hurt me," he said, "and you know that, and then you do it again. So at what point am I supposed to believe that you aren't doing it to take some sort of stand against me? Why do I feel like I'm being put in my place when all I'm doing is getting as close to you as you keep pushing me to?"

This was supposed to be easy. I'd been so sure of myself and so sure of him that I hadn't prepared for the inevitable. I was a selfish man with my own needs, and I had grossly underestimated what I'd feel for him and what it would mean to know him. I had truly believed that things—that he—would just fall into place. He had proven me wrong from day one, yet I still believed it would one day be so simple.

"Don't give up on me," I said, before I could close the door to vulnerability. I didn't speak this way, nor had I ever asked anyone not to leave me. I had watched many people walk out of my life—and made no attempt to prevent them from doing so. If anything, I'd been relieved to see them go. But with him, when I saw him hurting, I'd find myself digging as deeply as I could to find what I needed within myself to bring him back.

"I know who I am," I continued. "And I know that you and I are not the same, and that I don't always understand your pain, but please don't give up on me yet."

His expression was one of concern now. He looked tired, he looked confused, but more than that, he looked hurt for me rather than as a result of me. My words had made him sad, and I saw him search my eyes for everything he wanted to believe to be true. This was his way. No matter what state he was in or how angry he was, if he believed I was hurting, he'd throw it all aside and tend to me first. He couldn't help himself.

"I want more," he said gently. "If I'm going to get this caught up in someone and let it do this to me, I need more. I believe in this, I do, but I need your childish need to run from me to fuck itself."

I smiled and brushed his hair from his brow again. "Then I'll give you that."

"You don't know how," he said, touching my face briefly before resting his hand on my thigh. "You want to, but I don't think you really know what it takes to give. You have a very big heart—you don't hide it as well as you think you do. You're kind and you're funny and I adore you, but you're also vicious. I know you don't mean to be, but this ability to turn your back on me, it's brutal and I don't know what to do with it."

"And you're not vicious?" I asked, feeling wounded when all I wanted was to stay as close to him as I knew how. "You tell me I'm vicious, you tell me I don't know how to love, I don't know what it means to give? You aren't coming for my throat when you say these things?"

"Because I want you to care," he said, becoming frustrated. "I'm not an acquaintance to you. I'm not just your weekends, and you fucking know it. You pushed me until I felt for you, and now I feel everything for you and it's wrecking me and that should matter to you. I don't think you understand what it's like to feel this connected to you, inexplicably, and then have you sever it. It fucking hurts. This isn't about ignoring calls. This is about why you do it. This is about your need to run from me and what that could become down the road. What are you asking me to invest in here?"

I was at a loss, and he'd exhausted what little was left in him. I didn't agree with him that my tendencies were cause for this level of discourse, but clearly he felt things far differently than I could. He didn't look at me when he finally broke our silence.

"I love you," he said, his voice trembling. "I love you and this is the problem."

The world ground to a halt. I didn't dare speak for fear of getting this wrong. Thankfully, he continued, either unfazed by my silence or granting me a grace period.

"It doesn't make any sense," he said, turning to face me again. "We don't make sense. I spent a lot of time working on my anxiety and doing what I had to do to get stronger and to exist without needing someone else to hold my hand, and now here I am, back where I started. I let myself avoid making plans just in case you call because really, all I want to do is be with you too. I hate how it feels to admit that when I'm pretty fucking sure I know where this could end up, but I'd rather have you next to me inducing a panic attack than not have you next to me at all. And I worry about you. I fucking worry about you all the time. You stay up too late, you push yourself too hard, you isolate yourself sometimes, and no one around you seems to notice or care, but I do. I notice and I care and I need to know that you're okay and I want to make you happy and honestly, I don't know why. It's like something in me feels responsible for you and it's exhausting. This is exhausting. I want—"

"I love you too." I looked at him and took his chin in my hand. "This isn't how I imagined saying it, but I love you too."

I fell into his eyes as though sinking into an abyss from which I'd never emerge. And I wouldn't. I would never come back from this, from him. Had there been any small doubt about this prior to now, it had been vanquished with the words *I love you*.

"I know you'll question me when I say this, but I think I loved you before I knew you," I continued. "You do belong with me, and I don't care if it makes sense to you or not. You belong with me, and I love you."

He stared into me, looking as though he hadn't believed he'd hear the words back. He leaned in and kissed me then. It wasn't passionate. It wasn't a moment of true romance. It was a pact. With those words and that kiss, we'd fully bound ourselves to one another, and I didn't think I'd ever felt a happiness like this.

January 2024

I HAD SPENT the day locked away in the house. I'd had no need to shop, as people kept leaving food for me at the door. As though I were a prisoner. If he were here, he wouldn't have let me eat a bite of any of it before he'd determined each ingredient. Regardless, he'd steam a vegetable to accompany them. It wasn't motherly, the way he did this. It was love and it was care that, before meeting him, I'd never felt nor had any interest in accepting. It was as though he owned me, and he worked tirelessly to tend to his investment.

He had joked many times after moving here that he expected an onslaught of casseroles from the neighbourhood wives, and that all would be delivered in cookware we'd be obligated to return, and we'd then be trapped into countless insufferable social engagements. No casseroles had ever materialized, but throughout the four years we'd been here together, he'd still open the small mailbox at our front door periodically and jokingly say "Casserole?" followed by a vicious remark about how useless the neighbours were proving themselves to be. His humour wasn't for everyone, but he'd made me laugh even during his most trying days. He could take us into the darkest depths of our relationship and minutes later put a smile back on my face. The number of casseroles I was now receiving would piss him off to no end.

I'd barely cleaned, but I'd created no mess in the last four weeks merely shuffling around the house. I drank coffee and sparsely touched the food left for me. When I did, I ate it directly out of the containers with a fork, leaving me few dishes to wash. I did my laundry but still couldn't bring myself to wash his. I took stock of what was in the fridge with no intention of doing anything about it. I watched some food rot because some of it was for meals he'd been planning to prepare for us. I left it there as though he'd return any day and get me and the house back into working order. I was useless and I was fine with that.

My phone rang constantly, and I was unapologetic about not taking certain calls. I spoke to my family very little, his family even less, and friends would get nothing from me. I was taking them all for granted and I knew that, but I didn't care about that either. Knowing that the worst they could do was stop calling wasn't a threat. It would have been a relief. I worked through our wine stash, which he'd curated, but managed to abstain until the evening hours. I didn't actually want its release during the day. I wanted to feel this loneliness, and I wanted every memory of him to remain vivid.

When darkness fell, however, it was too much to take. The emptiness terrified me. He wasn't in the kitchen preparing us dinner while chattering at me. He wasn't in the basement working out, counting every minute he was down there to ensure he didn't fall short. He wasn't showering, his music filling the upstairs while I strained to make out the sound of him quietly singing along. He wasn't here, and the nights were cold and silent without him. The sights and sounds of people going about their day outside the house faded by early evening, leaving me inside of our home with no reminder that the world was in fact still turning.

Tonight, I'd chosen to stay on the main level with my wine. I gazed out the front window, as he had so often done. I didn't want to leave the house, but being able to turn my back on the emptiness of it and see the outdoors sometimes helped. I stared into the darkness. The winter had stripped our front yard of its charm, and the streetlights cast a glow that felt more like an echo in the absence of any life. The house was cold, but I didn't touch the thermostat. The idea of warming myself filled me with immense guilt. Why should I be comfortable in our home after he'd endured such pain? Why should it even feel like home when it was he who'd made it one?

I placed my glass on the floor beside the couch and wrapped my arms around my shins, my chin on my knees. A shiver had crept up the length of my spine, and I struggled not to respond. I held myself tightly and felt incapacitating grief begin its nightly descent on me. He wouldn't want this. He wouldn't want me this way. He would have thrown a blanket around me and told me to stop trying to prove something. He would have reminded me that it was okay to show weakness. That it was okay to hurt.

I closed my eyes and envisioned him crossing the living room and climbing on top of me to smother me. I imagined the way he'd try to cover every inch of my body with his and then bury his face in my neck. He did this even before we owned a couch that could fit us both, and I cherished it. The feel of him, the scent of him. He sometimes seemed like a wild animal that had chosen me as its mate.

The daydream had caused me to let my guard down, and my body shook from the chill. A lump formed in my throat but, as always, tears didn't follow. I considered going to bed, but the thought of being there without him another night hollowed me, so there I sat cold and alone in the centre of our home. I buried my face deeper into my knees and sniffled, my nose beginning to run. I closed my eyes and was wondering how much lower I could slide into this state, when I heard an unmistakable sound: a small gust of wind followed by a light tapping.

I opened my eyes and slowly raised my head. The gas fireplace, directly across from me, had ignited, and the flames burned at full strength. I froze for several moments, puzzled. How could this have happened? Turning it on required lifting the switch tucked on the left side of the fireplace itself, and I was more than two metres from it.

Before my mind could wander, I uncoiled myself, stood from the couch, and walked to the fireplace. If he were here, he would have forced us to take a moment to acknowledge the peculiarity of this. Inevitably, he would have suggested that *something* had turned it on. I didn't share his beliefs, and had no room for these considerations now. My fingers fumbled along the frame of the fireplace before finding the switch, only to discover that it was in its correct position. I moved it up and down multiple times, but the flames remained. I straightened, crossed my arms, and stared down at the fire for several moments.

It was cruel. Anger filled me. I returned to the couch and downed half of the wine in my glass in one sip. Countless winter weekends, he'd made himself a drink, then sat next to the fire and absorbed its heat while engaging me in lightly drunken conversation. Usually, we'd rehash our week at work together. He wasn't sitting by the fireplace now, and my emotions were at the mercy of a malfunction to which I saw no solution.

The warmth touched my feet and then slowly travelled the length of my body before settling on my face. I reluctantly began to feel almost at ease. The discomfort I'd committed to enduring was giving way to a sense of home. Far more quickly than I'd thought possible given my recent insomnia, I drifted off.

Hours later I woke to find that I'd spilled my wine across the couch. A large red stain had been permanently absorbed into the beige fabric. I felt disgust toward myself for a moment before just as quickly remembering it didn't matter. Nothing did. The fire had gone out, the room was cold again, and I felt the misery of knowing that I'd now make my way to our bedroom. I looked around and, for the hundredth time that day, felt consumed by the emptiness of our home. He would never again climb onto me here on this couch and use the weight of his body to warm me, to remind me to whom I belonged.

Unsteadily, I pulled myself up and was overcome with a sudden rage. Without thinking, I threw my wineglass across the room and watched it shatter against the wall. I screamed into the silence that followed and put my head in my hands, waiting for the tears to fall. They held firm.

Catching my breath, I felt both self-pity and anger over my actions. I looked down at the mess I'd made, my chest heaving. I needed something, anything to let me know that this wasn't real and that he'd come around the corner now and demand to know why I'd done this. I needed a sign that he'd soon be home, and he'd help me clean up the pieces of what was left behind. It didn't come—it never would—and I slowly made my way up the stairs to our room with my head hung, leaving the floor littered with glass and the large burgundy stain on our couch untouched.

Walking into the bedroom, I was filled with the sickness I'd come to feel every night when I made myself cross this threshold. But tonight, something was different. Instead of feeling just cold and empty, the room also felt familiar again. Had my brief emotional outburst provided some unexpected release? I wasn't prepared to give the idea any weight. Knowing this feeling was temporary, I dismissed it and stripped off my clothes. Before crawling into bed, I passed his window and, for the first time in a month, felt compelled to stop at it. But I didn't. I sat on the edge of the bed in my underwear, forcing myself to eradicate thoughts of the fireplace, the wine I'd spilled, and the shattered glass that would be waiting for me in the morning.

I wouldn't waste an ounce of energy on the mess I'd made. I didn't care. He would say that I was a master at turning my back, but he never understood how hard I'd worked at that. This thought lingered with me: the memory of his frustration over my refusal to succumb to anger, sadness, or depression. What would he think of me now? Would it make him happy to see me in such undeniable suffering? Would he consider it good for me? I wanted him here, challenging me. I'd hated how he'd corner me into these dialogues, but now I'd have given anything to fight with him about this, about anything. I wanted to hear him without taking for granted what he was saying and how he knew me. I wanted him and the complicated, exhausting, and often infuriating emotional rigour he put me through.

I wanted him so badly in that moment, I believed it might kill me. The ache was unbearable. I clenched my fists in my lap and squeezed my eyes shut, feeling ready. I was ready to let it consume me. I would set fire to this house and stand in the centre of it as it burned. This wasn't a home. It never would be again. I inhaled, bracing myself to scream, but instead caved in under the weight of it all. My breath left me, my shoulders slouched, my head once again hung under its own weight. I unclenched my fists and choked back a whimper as a shudder ran through me. There was nothing ahead of me without him. I prayed for something to take me, if not to him, then away from everything else.

My eyes still shut, I sensed movement in the room then. Something to my left had stirred. The hairs on my arms stood on end. I opened my eyes and my heart left my body as I realized I'd been right. Without turning my head, I looked toward his window, which was closed. The thin white curtains we'd hung were moving in a breeze felt only by them. I watched in disbelief, unmoving. I closed my eyes, sure that when I opened them again, I'd discover that all was as it should be. I turned my head toward the window and slowly lifted my eyelids.

There he stood. My love. Not a vision of him, not the sense of him I'd pleaded for.

Him.

He was naked, gazing out into the night beyond, his hands resting on the window ledge. The moonlight cast a glow on his face and chest, and the curtains gently flowed around him, occasionally passing themselves over his pale skin. This wasn't grief and this wasn't the short-term effects of insomnia. He was here—his face, his body, his energy—unscathed. Without breathing, I let my eyes move from his face, down his spine, across the curve of his backside, and along the length of his legs.

I was frozen, but my heart was beating so quickly I thought I might lose consciousness. My eyes filled with tears. Whatever was happening, I was overwhelmed by the cruelty of it—but more so by love. The love I had lost flooded back into me. It was as though it had never died. It ran through me like poison, killing off any reason or sound judgment. I had never seen him more beautiful.

Seconds passed. He hadn't moved. My gaze returned to his face as the tears that had evaded me finally ran down my cheeks. I wanted to speak his name, but couldn't, for fear he'd leave. That it would somehow shatter what was happening and he'd be no more. Needing oxygen, my body forced me to take a sharp inhale. As the sound escaped me, his head turned so slowly in my direction that I began wondering if I had been wrong, if he was in fact a hallucination. Eventually his eyes reached mine. We locked our gazes. His movements were soundless. It seemed he was existing in a place where time had slowed. His head tilted pensively to the right, his eyes still on mine. His expression was one of sorrow, and he was looking down at me as though feeling my agony. His lips slowly parted, and the voice that had once soothed any pain I had ever known, even that which it had inflicted, softly spoke.

"My love," he said, barely above a whisper.

My body recoiled on the bed as my nervous system collapsed. A sound of terror escaped me. His hands slowly fell from the window ledge and then hung at his sides. He turned his body toward me and his expression darkened. He looked wounded by my reaction. I swallowed and could barely see through my tears. My entire body shook. It was as lost as my mind about how to respond to what was happening. Slowly, his foot lifted, and he took a step toward me. The love I had felt upon seeing him was now eclipsed by fear, and without wanting to, I screamed, recoiling further.

And then he was gone. The curtains settled into place and fell still. I looked around the room in desperation, panting, tears pouring down my cheeks. Despite the dread that had consumed me just seconds ago, I was searching for him. I sat up, my hands still planted on the mattress. I looked back toward the window, and though I couldn't see him, he remained. I could feel him all over me. I began to sob. My body heaved, and I buried my head between my knees.

2013

"I DON'T NEED you," he said, with venom. "I don't fucking need you, and I don't need this."

He was shoving his clothes into his overnight bag, looking around to ensure he'd left nothing behind. I was sitting on the edge of the bed in my condo, believing that if I remained calm, he'd eventually allow me to reason with him. This wasn't our first argument, but it might have been the most upset I'd ever seen him.

"Please stop," I said, looking up at him as he slung his bag over his shoulder.

He did stop, but apparently not because he was having second thoughts. He had parting words. "What is it about you that makes you think you can treat me like this? Am I supposed to be so fucking flattered by your interest in me that I'll just tolerate it?"

I closed my eyes. "Of course not."

"Then what?" he snapped. "What the fuck is it about you that makes you think you're worth this? What the fuck just happened here?"

I had no answer. Whatever I'd envisioned we'd be, I'd done so without having any idea of who he was or what his needs were. I'd expected him to conform, and over a year into our relationship I was still doing it. I was hurting him, often, and he was revealing himself to be far more emotionally unsteady than I knew how to manage.

I'd had a work engagement the previous evening to which I'd initially asked him to accompany me. At the last minute, I became uncomfortable with the idea of having my work life and personal life intersect and decided it was best that he not come. He had questions, and I tried in my way to talk through it with him, but ultimately, I held firm. Thinking it best not to have him sit home alone that evening, his wheels turning, I asked him to meet me at my place, where we'd spend the remainder of the night together. The very idea of having him there when I came home made me happy, and he obliged.

He had my key, the doorman knew him, and I insisted that he'd be there alone only a short while. Time got away from me at the event, and when I arrived home well after midnight, I found a photo of us, which he'd had framed for me, in ruin. He'd thrown the framed image against the wall, then pulled out the photo, torn it in two, and left it amongst the shattered glass. Other than this carnage and an empty bottle of wine, there was no sign of him, but his overnight bag was still sitting on my bed.

I hadn't tried to find him. My phone showed several missed calls from him, none of which I'd returned. Hubris or simply genuine trust told me he'd be back for his belongings the next day—he'd left that window open—so I went to bed exhausted and prepared to deal with it then. It wasn't so much my fear of confrontation as it was my inability to explain myself or any of my decisions that evening.

I folded my hands in my lap, nodding. "You're right," I said. "I should have called."

I'd believed I'd chosen my words carefully, but the rage that immediately swallowed his eyes told me I hadn't.

"It was one in the morning when I left," he said, gnashing his teeth. "I was here waiting for you, in your home, as you'd asked me to, for four hours. And the worst part is that the humiliation of being uninvited to your event didn't even set in until I'd sat here staring at your walls long enough."

"You should feel perfectly at home here."

"I have my own fucking home with my own fucking bed," he shot back. "That isn't what this is about, and you know it. I'm not a new fucking lamp. You can't station me here because you think I suit the place, and then wash your hands of me. Do you understand how weak you make me look? Spending a night locked away and waiting for you after you'd decided that, clearly, I'm not cut out to have been there with you?"

I closed my eyes again. "Okay," I said, with deliberate calm. "I think you're taking this a bit far. I'm not washing my hands of you. I very much wanted you here when I got back, and I—"

"But not with you, even though everyone else there would have had their partner next to them. I'm suitable here, or tucked away in a dark bar or at least a good distance from coworkers and their families because I couldn't possibly hold my own—"

"It wasn't important."

"It was important to me!" he yelled. "I thought I was getting somewhere with you, and for the first time I actually felt like you were proud of me, like I fucking belonged with you. I'm letting you do this to me and it's making me sick and you're not even within the realm of understanding why that is. This or something just like it keeps happening. You have me where you fucking want me and so no more effort required, right?"

My patience was waning, and the me that had existed before him was taking the reins. "You've got me all figured out, yes?" I said, looking up at him blankly. "I'm the monster to your perpetual victim and I deserve no further consideration. You can fly off the handle at me every time you feel hurt, but I'm not allowed to explain to you, for the hundredth time, that I process things much differently than you do."

He glared at me as though accepting a challenge. "Process things?" he asked, almost menacingly. "Pretty hard to process something when your first course of action is to turn your back on it like a scared child."

"And you're any better?" I shot back. "Because it looks to me like the empty bottle of wine you left in the kitchen did the heavy lifting for you, again."

"Shut up."

"Or maybe I should take a cue from the manner in which you processed trauma, by fellating your way through your home-town at age seventeen?" I said, sickened with myself as soon as the words left my mouth.

He was taken aback by this. I didn't speak to him this way and we both knew that. Without warning, he pulled his bag from his shoulder and threw it with force against the closet door. I flinched as though I'd been struck and went rigid in anticipation of what he'd say or do next. I was in over my head. I didn't want this. I wanted him, but I didn't want this. There'd been a handful of these fights now, and all had ended with an explosive outburst from him and then fierce lovemaking. This wasn't healthy, and we both knew it, but I believed that the eventual sex solidified our connection. The afterglow gave us time to sort through the mess of us, and we always did. But the fights had never brought me to the point of wanting to intentionally harm him, and now I had.

Afraid to look him in the eyes, I kept my face down. "I'm sorry," I said. "That was disgusting of me, and I am so sorry." I risked a glance at him. "You're pushing me to the brink here." I hadn't intended to blame him, though it was true. This level of warfare wasn't something to which I was accustomed.

"This isn't working," he said, breathing heavily but trying to calm himself. "I hate myself like this, and I'm making you hate me too."

I watched him give way to the exhaustion he was obviously feeling. Undoubtedly, he hadn't slept. He hung his head, and his arms moved to his chest as it heaved, his anxiety beginning to launch its own battle against him.

Neither of us spoke for a time, and when he did, his face remained pointed toward the floor and his tone was heavy. "You make me hate myself."

My brow furrowed. "Don't say that—"

"I don't know why we both want this so badly when it just keeps ending the same way. I don't think I can fix it. I'm sorry." His voice shook. "I don't understand us, and I don't think I can do it anymore."

I considered this. He handled his pain horribly, with destruction and rage, but he was rarely wrong. We were supposed to be beautiful and instead we had become toxic. Only I couldn't admit it. It might have been time to give up the fight, but I wouldn't. Not ever. Whatever fantasy I'd had about a life together had spiraled into this chaos, but I felt certain this would pass and we could try once more.

I stared up at him, taking him in. I knew he was suffering. His breathing was deliberate as he staved off an attack. Seeing him this way made me want to run from everything I didn't understand, but more than that, it made me want to save him. Even if I was the one who'd gotten him to this place.

I slowly reached out to take his hand and he allowed me to, tears rolling down his cheek. "I never, ever try to hurt you," I said. "I'm so sorry for what I just said to you, and we both know you didn't deserve it, so don't go telling yourself that you did. I respect you. I do, a great deal."

He raised his eyes to me, and I was relieved to see how much his anger had subsided. "I think I know that. But the way you refuse to treat me like I'm your equal ..."

"You are my equal."

"No," he said. "You wouldn't have severed me from your life last night if you believed that. There is your life and then there is mine, and it's clear to me that my priorities come a distant second to yours."

I wanted to argue, but again, he wasn't entirely wrong. I admired him in many ways, but the differences between us often made it feel as though one of us had to lose in order to move forward, and he believed it was always him. I didn't want that for him, but I couldn't save him from himself. I believed it to be his own fault that he allowed things to affect him the way he did, and early in our relationship I'd developed a tendency to watch him unravel rather than show him enough consideration or compassion to intervene. All I seemed able to do was wait for the storm to pass and hope to get us back on track. Ultimately, he would decide that every time.

"You wanted this," he said, looking weary. "You've told me how many times that you believe you and I are meant to be something? You push me away then show up at my door. You shut me out then demand to be glued to me every other spare waking moment—"

"I've heard this all before—"

"Then why am I still saying it?" he asked, anger returning to his tone.

He watched me, waiting for a response, but I had none. The picture he'd painted made me ashamed. I wanted it all, but I hadn't yet grasped the cost of it.

"I still believe that," I said cautiously. I spoke slowly, hoping my thoughts would form in time for me to provide him with something worthy of consideration. "I know you question it, and I know I give you good reason to." He wasn't interrupting me, so I continued. "I wish that you understood how I feel for you and how important you are to my life—"

"Give me reason to believe it and I will. I want to."

"We see things differently," I said, nervous but entitled to a role in this fight. "I know you're hurt, but I didn't and wouldn't ever do that to you deliberately."

"But you do this shit knowing that it is going to hurt me. That's not deliberate?" He pulled his hand from mine and crossed his arms, but he sounded less angry and more rational. "You act like an arrogant kid who thinks he can pay off his mistakes with flowers and a kind word or two about the way I look today." He was pushing his point, but his will was subsiding. "This is how I imagine professional athletes treat their girlfriends after a night of cocaine and blow jobs." He paused and a small smile, the promise of peace, began to fight its way into his lips. He sniffled and wiped away a tear that had threatened him moments ago. "Were you out doing cocaine and getting blow jobs?"

Thank god. We were moving forward. He had a checkered past, and I'd never touched a drug in my life. We understood that about each other and respected the different paths we'd taken. I was assured now that he was coming back around to me and that he wanted to see me smile.

"Just the cocaine," I said with a shrug.

"I fucking knew it," he said, his eyes narrowing. He stifled a laugh.

He looked down and twisted his foot nervously on the floor, biting his cheek. "I mean it," he said, looking up at me again, one determined tear running down his cheek. "I'm just not built for this, for you. It turns out I'm needy and I'm codependent and I don't have your strength. Also, I'm maybe a touch insecure."

I smiled and again appreciated his injection of humour into what I hoped was the end of this fight.

"I love you," he said. "I really do."

I reached up and took his hand again, this time pulling him gently onto the bed with me. "You're not going anywhere," I said, and held his hand in my lap. "You belong here with me, and I truly believe that. I know we don't see things the same way, and I know it's challenging for you sometimes."

"Condescending," he said, turning his head to me, his confidence restoring itself.

Before this took another turn, I leaned in and kissed him. I could sense he was fighting with himself, part of him wishing he'd had the strength to leave. The part of him that remained kissed me back and, as he did, every muscle in my body unwound. When I pulled away, I took his head in my hands and looked into his eyes. I paused and ran a finger down his cheek.

"You and me, right?" I asked. "We're going to figure this out, but I need you to stay."

He ran a finger down my cheek as well, watching his own movement. He was tired and he was angry but beneath all of that, what he needed—what we both needed—was each other. After every argument, what we needed was each other. Separation made no sense. Minutes later our clothes were off, and we were both reminded of how right it felt being close to one another. Nothing had ever made me feel this way, and I would fight for it until it killed me.

February 2024

FEBRUARY MOVED IN at midnight, and the following morning, I found that a blizzard had ground life outdoors to a halt. It was the type of day that had never seemed to land on our time off, when we would have relished the opportunity to watch a storm wreak havoc outside from the warmth of our sanctuary together. We had loved storms, and both seemed to get a charge from their approach.

I hadn't slept. At some point in the night, I'd finally gotten under the covers, where I'd lain shaking until dawn. I had stared, mostly unblinking, at his window. I'd wanted him to return, but if he had, it might have been the death of me. I allowed his visit to replay itself over and over. Every time my traumatized mind began to stray, I snapped myself back to ensure that I kept every second of it as accurate and vivid as possible. I'd spent many hours of these weeks praying to a power I didn't believe in that he would come back to me, and now he had. I would hold on to this with whatever sacrifice to my belief system it would require, aware that this could very well be the beginning of my unravelling. I didn't believe these things possible, but I'd also never believed in anything the way I'd believed in him.

Early morning I'd moved downstairs and resumed my position on the wine-stained couch, ignoring the glass scattered about the floor. I stared out the window and watched the wind violently toss snow in whatever direction it chose minute to minute. It was a carbon copy of the day he'd died. As the sun rose, it had revealed a morning just like this, and I'd stared out at it from the window of a hospital room. The room in which I'd been placed looked out over the very woods I'd just been dragged from. I'd stared out that window, numb to everything happening around me, waiting for him to emerge from the trees.

I didn't fight this memory of his death, as I often did. I allowed it to slide to the forefront of my mind, and with it came the vivid recount of what had obliterated our happiness. I let myself be reminded of the kiss I hadn't returned that morning, of his long, lean body moving effortlessly through the snow, framed by the woods on either side of him. I let the image of his face, looking over his shoulder at me, flushed and wet, carve a new hole into my heart.

For a moment my instincts attempted to rebuild my mental barrier before I went too far, but then I surrendered. I saw the animal drag him from the trail and trample his body with utter disregard for what it was taking from me. I watched the blood flow from his body while he spent those last moments trying to remain connected to me. He hadn't fought death, I later realized; he'd used his remaining fire to give me what he always had: unwavering commitment and a promise through those eyes that I'd never be without him. It's what I'd chosen to believe.

His return to me the previous night solidified that promise, and though the terror I'd felt hearing his voice lingered, it had left behind a feeling more carnal. I couldn't explain it to myself, but the more I'd replayed it, the more it aroused me. Through the tears, the devastation, and the fear, I'd felt close to him in a way that was reminiscent of what I'd experienced every time I'd been naked next to him. I was disgusted with myself for it, but it was persistent.

He's not here now, I reminded myself. What I'd seen in the moonlight hadn't materialized into his absolute return, and therefore, it couldn't have been as real as my broken heart had believed in that moment. I was becoming embarrassed of myself. My head was now deep in battle, and I made no effort to intervene nor choose sides. I didn't know what to believe anymore.

My eyes burned, and despite my lack of movement, my body ached and I felt nauseated and weak. I needed to sleep, and I wondered if, after his countless sleepless nights, he'd felt this way, yet still forged on for me. My stomach rumbled, reminding me that I also hadn't eaten properly in some time. My grief had become more than a period of mourning—it was devouring me.

Feeling too weak to attempt to move from the couch in search of food, I let my head fall back onto the cushion. The room spun, and a shudder ran through me as I realized I was going to pass out. I fought it in vain. Just before the room went dark, I heard the fireplace turn on. In anticipation of its warmth, I felt a sense of reassurance, and then sleep found me again.

I dreamt for the first time in weeks. I was standing at the opening of the trail on which he'd seen his last morning. It loomed ahead of me, enticing me to come through, but I stood motionless. The snow fell as wildly as it had fallen and the wind blew as it had blown, the only sound to break the silence. It was daylight, but the sun was nowhere to be found. Though a storm raged around me, I felt no cold. I felt nothing at all.

I considered the trail before me but knew that ultimately, I had no choice but to move through it. It was as though the world at my back had vanished and all I could do was push myself forward into the uncertainty that lay ahead. I began to walk clumsily through the snow, with no path having been forged by other travellers. It was difficult, but sensation gradually returned to my body and my muscles responded accordingly. My legs became stronger by the second, helping me to steady myself despite the lack of support underfoot. As I pushed through the snow, my pace quickened to a light jog. I knew I was dreaming because my legs, my ankle, never would have allowed for this without faltering. I felt strong and I felt determined, as though I knew that something awaited me down the path.

The trees felt like an enclosure as I entered the trail, their branches exaggerated and creating a dark, leafless ceiling above me. They provided the same shelter we'd sometimes known, but in this place they felt unwelcoming. Still, I continued, and the further in I ran, the faster I began to move. I ran until I was at a pace I hadn't achieved in some years. I didn't struggle. I could hear my breath, the wind, the snow underneath me, yet I felt nothing other than my legs working on my behalf.

The snow was nearly blinding, but ahead I noticed something to the right of the trail. I held my gaze on the figure as I approached. The blowing snow prevented me from making out the details of the form, but I knew what this was. The wind swirled into a chaotic fury around me, but I didn't slow. The heart inside my dreaming body quickened as the snow intensified. I was now merely a few feet from him. I moved with a sense of desperation as I closed the gap between us.

Just as I was about to reach him, he launched into a run at a pace equal to mine. A surge of adrenaline coursed through me, and I pushed myself to reach him before I woke. Try as I might, I couldn't catch him. I pushed but began to lose my footing, and my breathing became laboured. Panic took hold of me as my body reminded me of its limitations, and I knew I could not reach him. But just as the defeat began to rise in my stomach, his legs began to slow.

He allowed me to catch up, and within seconds he was next to me. We were side by side, pushing through the storm, the road ahead becoming more treacherous and the snow now blinding me completely. I doubted how much farther I could go, but he extended his arm and traced his finger down the length of my spine, sending a current of electricity pulsing through me. I turned my head to look at him, expecting to see him smiling at me, encouraging me, but he was gone. I ran alone through the storm, everything around me suddenly feeling sinister and unfamiliar.

I slowed, then stumbled to a halt as I felt my body trying to wake itself. I stood panting when ahead of me, he suddenly reappeared on the trail, cutting through the snow and running toward me. He'd emerged from the very spot in the woods that the wolf had dragged him to, made a sharp turn back onto the trail, and was now coming at me at an impossible speed. I no longer felt the comfort of him next to me and instead felt the terror that had seized me when he'd spoken my name the night before. His movement felt hostile, and I took a step backward, instinct telling me to turn and run in the opposite direction. As soon as I tried to do so, I tripped over something and stumbled, sprawling out on my stomach across the snow. Feeling the cold on my face, I immediately scrambled to pull myself up and turned onto my back, lifting myself onto my elbows.

When I awoke on the couch, the image of what lay between my legs, sprawled out in the snow, came with me. He was no longer running toward me but was here, his throat pouring blood, his arm bent at an impossible angle and barely attached to his body. His eyes faced the sky, but in the last seconds before

I regained consciousness in our living room, they looked toward me and, through his bloodstained lips, in a broken voice I'd heard through his tears time and time again, he said, "I'm sorry."

I woke screaming the words, "I'm sorry!"

I bolted upright, disoriented and struggling to catch my breath. The fire still burned, and the storm still raged outside. Tears began to flow, and I took several deep breaths, slowly slumping back into the couch, my body shivering.

"I'm sorry," I whimpered. "Baby, I'm so sorry."

2014

We ran side by side along the river with the city at our backs. This was the only portion of our Saturday runs that didn't require us to navigate busy sidewalks or ill-timed traffic lights. On this stretch, we could stay close. With music in our ears, we'd periodically allow our arms to graze as we moved, a reminder that we hadn't forgotten each other.

The Christmas season was ahead of us, but as was typical in this city, no snow had fallen. This didn't matter to us. In my time with him, he'd helped me to rediscover the season and enjoy it—the decor, the movies, the overindulgence, the time with chosen families. He was spending more nights than not with me, and together we'd purchased a tree and made a project of handpicking its ornaments, all of which ended up being woodland animals of some sort. There were creative differences; I preferred a classic approach that would complement my space, whereas he aimed to recapture the image of his childhood Christmases. He didn't often speak kindly of that period in his life, and I didn't want him to sacrifice those memories, so we met halfway.

I caught the sound of him singing quietly as we ran, and lowered the volume of my music to make out what tune had inspired him. I laughed under my breath when I realized it was a Christmas carol. While other gay men his age had embraced club culture and were holding on to it for what remaining years they could, he was working out to holiday music or listening to the sounds of the 1970s. I didn't understand how someone so riddled with anxiety, depression, and bad memories could share a headspace with this creature who at times exuded such joy. The worst was that it was rubbing off on me. Never one to show more signs of exuberance than necessary, I now joined him in concert and followed suit when he added a well-timed step or hand gesture to the performance. He made me happy. Despite our hurdles, he was making me so happy.

We were still experiencing bumps in our road together, and I'd come to accept that this might always be. He responded strongly when he felt threatened or believed that I'd hurt him, and I remained unproperly equipped to address these situations, though I continued to try. Sadly, it had settled into somewhat of a pattern, but these days in between were joy to me, and the more months of his life he gave me, the more I wanted. He was worth every fight, and I'd begun to feel that the future I'd envisioned for us was in fact possible.

That evening, we sat on my couch, nursing some wine. He was pressed so tightly against me that I feared I'd fall over its arm if I didn't engage every required muscle to prevent it. These evenings with him provided me more warmth than I'd ever known, and I adored how ridiculous he was about insisting he needed to be this close to me. If he'd released me and allowed me to rest comfortably with adequate space, I would surely have missed him and pulled him back.

"Do you hate the tree?" he asked, taking a sip.

I was caught off guard somewhat, but not entirely. I knew never to assume where his mind was at simply because his body suggested he was present.

"No, you idiot," I said. "I love our tree."

He laughed and nudged me. "You're the idiot who wanted that star, so I'm just saying."

"Just saying what?"

"That if you hate the tree, that star is likely why and maybe you should consider that before you come at me about how this is, like, the worst Christmas you've ever had and this tree will forever remind you of what we'll always refer to as *Dark Christmas*." He nodded in approval, staring at our tree. "Maybe you should think about that next time you insist that your fancy ass knows best because you don't, I do, and on Boxing Day that star is going to meet its maker."

He took another sip of his wine, and as soon as it was safe, I took the glass from his hand and placed it on the glass coffee table.

"Hey," he protested.

Smiling, I shifted and pushed him playfully onto his back.

He reached for the glass again. "But I want it more than I want you!" he cried.

I laughed and pinned him down with the weight of my body, burying myself into him until he finally succumbed and wrapped his arms around me. I outweighed him by a good twenty pounds of muscle, and he often made an exaggerated point of sounding as though he were being crushed beneath me, never admitting to his own strength. I gently kissed his neck and brushed his hair from his forehead.

"Thank you," he said quietly. "For this."

I turned my head so that we were cheek to cheek.

"For what?" I asked.

He exhaled in annoyance, realizing that I needed him to explain his feelings to me.

"This is the first time I've enjoyed Christmas this much in a really long time," he said. "I wish we could both just stay here like this."

We'd talked about spending the holidays together but, neither of us prepared to disappoint family, decided that we were still new enough to excuse each other's absences one last Christmas. We behaved as though we had nothing but time, and that the slow and often painful path we'd taken still lay open ahead of us. I would have had no problem travelling home with him, but he struggled a great deal with family, and the idea of immersing himself in another one made him near frantic, so I hadn't pushed him yet. I felt secure enough with him in this moment, though, that I decided I was ready to broach another subject we'd lightly touched on several times and that he'd been quick to dismiss.

"You know," I began, "what would make that a little easier would be you never having to leave at all."

I felt his body tighten beneath me, but he didn't respond.

"I don't like it," I continued. "I don't like the mornings when you pack your bag and leave, and I don't like the weeknights when you feel you can't stay because you don't want to sacrifice your routines. I don't like what it feels like when you leave here. It's empty."

He was about to respond but I kept going, wanting to keep the door open and to argue my case. "And I completely respect how important routine is to you, and I know that it affects your anxiety when things aren't planned or you feel you've lost time." His body softened slightly, and I sustained my momentum. "So, imagine the time you'd save if you didn't have to go home and get ready before beginning your day. What if this was home and everything you needed was right here?"

Silence. I'd opened myself to him, as I continued to try to do, and he'd met me with silence.

After a few moments he gently used the required strength to push me off him, and I rolled to his side, my leg keeping him pinned and my arm wrapped around him to secure him from falling off the couch. He didn't fight me, but he didn't face me. He stared across the room at our tree.

"I know that you want that," he said calmly, placing his hand over his eyes as though he could shield himself from hurting me. "And I don't want you to misunderstand why I don't."

A small pin tapped the surface of my heart. This wasn't going to end the way I'd hoped. I should have known better. I was ruining an otherwise perfect evening, and he'd undoubtably want to leave when this was over.

"Once we do that, there's no going back," he continued.

"I wouldn't want there to be," I replied, grabbing his chin and turning his face toward mine.

"Right," he said, removing his hand from his eyes and looking into mine. "And then a year down the road, you look at me and realize there's nowhere to go from here. There's no mystery between us, we argue over who should clean the bathroom, we gain weight, and we slowly die."

"Okay, come on—"

"No, you need to think about this." He held my gaze, but his eyes had fallen dark. "I mean no disrespect, but when you and your exes separated, what was happening? Had you not given up on each other over time and then both decided that you needed to get out and find life again?"

He was right, of course. For someone who'd crash-landed into love time and time again, he had acute observations of it from the outside.

"That was a different time and those were different relation-ships," I offered. "Those years have nothing to do with the future I see with you."

He touched my face before pulling his own from my hand. He truly didn't want to hurt me, and I could see how much this conversation was paining him.

"But that's what will happen," he insisted. "Any couple who denies that is lying. They all come to resent one another. They miss the life and the independence they had before they fooled themselves into believing their relationship would be different. Ours won't, and I have no interest in that. I'm sorry. It hurts too fucking much."

This was, perhaps, the most unexplainable thing about us. Admittedly I was responsible for every single time that I'd closed myself to him and pushed him away. I had broken him many times with my refusal to fold and allow him to pull me into his emotional hurricane, and that likely wouldn't change. Yet, he was solely responsible for the distance between us that would never be closed. I wanted him near me always, and despite his fury on the nights he felt I was withdrawn from him, he'd main-tain this space whenever I attempted to close it.

I was saddened. I hadn't taken time to assess why he might feel so opposed to living here with me. I wanted the prospect to be joyful. I brushed his hair from his forehead and gently kissed his cheek. He was damaged, as we all were, and he'd developed his own coping mechanisms. Though I wanted to be angry, I also needed to admit to myself that we weren't always so different. What he was doing now was no different from what I'd done to him time and time again.

"We are different, though," I said, as I took his chin in my hand again and held his gaze. "We are. I don't believe for one second that you and I would ever reach that place."

His eyes were moistening, but I didn't panic. This often happened as he sorted through things within himself, and more often than not, he came out the other side in working order.

"I love you so much," he said. "More than you know, I think, and I really want you to be happy because you make me happy. It doesn't always seem like it, but you do. You make me so happy when I'm with you."

I smiled, already knowing this to be true, but the sting in my heart deepened as I watched his expression firm.

"I don't trust you, though," he said. "And what will happen if one night you don't come home and I have no choice but to be here, waiting for you, with nowhere to go. I would be at your mercy, and I can't do that. I can't do that to myself, and I'm sorry. I'm so sorry."

I wanted to pretend this was a fabricated concern, but this was all stemming from the many tumultuous days and nights we'd had together. From the times I'd left him for hours, waiting for me, his insecurities running amok. From the times he'd opened himself to me, been vulnerable, and I'd been unable to reciprocate. I wasn't responsible for his past, but it was a part of him, and it angered me how it misguided the strength he possessed. If he could recalibrate and direct this energy toward a positive outlook, he might see us differently. He was to be held accountable for his emotions and how they dictated his responses, but equally, I was to be held accountable for the hole that I worried would now always exist between us. We felt hopeless in these moments.

"I'm not asking you to marry me—"

"I can't give you this," he said. "I love you and I would give my life to save yours, but I can't give you this."

"I can't make sense of that. And what does that mean for us? What does forward look like to you if sharing a home isn't ever going to be on the table?"

He pulled himself to a seated position, leaving me where we'd both lay cuddling moments ago. He looked down at me and tried to smile, but quickly turned away.

"I don't know," he said quietly. "I can't explain myself any better than you can." He turned his head and looked down into my eyes again, his expression sad. "I feel like I should leave now, but it would kill me if I tried. I don't understand it either and I'm sorry."

I stared at him a moment before I roughly pulled him on top of me and kissed him passionately.

February 2024

I HAD PULLED apart every box I'd found in the closet beneath the basement stairs. We hadn't kept photo albums, but memories of us existed in frames, tucked away into books, on shelves throughout the house, and on our phones. I hadn't sought access to his phone, though. And I wouldn't. There was nothing about him that I could learn from its contents that would help me. Worse, if there was anything there that he hadn't wanted me to know, then I didn't want to know it. So, I was left with the memories he'd deemed worthy of printing. And I'd come across a shoebox that held exactly that.

We'd been together several years before we travelled together, but when we did, we discovered that we were, in fact, a remarkable team. There were photos of us standing on volcanoes, trekking through rainforests, and posing in front of monuments he'd had no interest in seeing but had visited for my sake. When we finally started to find calm in our relationship, we'd been able to focus on actually sharing a life rather than on picking up the pieces of a morning after. His mental illness had dictated so much of what he felt he could or couldn't do in life, and these photos reminded me of how hard he'd pushed himself to make sure we had these experiences together.

He'd channelled his anxiety and his need to establish plans into mapping out every minute of every journey. He made travel arrangements. He scoured all resources to find us the best hotels with budget, location, and aesthetic in mind. He located the best restaurants, the most obscure sites, and he did everything he could to plan us a trip that would differ from that of anyone who'd been to the same location. He refused to take tours— we shared that stipulation—so we created our own, which took us away from any and all expectations and made the experiences raw and unpredictable. He'd lead us out of bounds, but his anxiety would always know when it was time to pull back, and he protected us from ever going too far. We were amazing together; we were a team, and we needed no one else.

I spread some of the photos from the shoebox out on the carpet, where I knelt. I didn't know what I was looking for. Until now, I'd been too afraid to do this. I still felt unprepared for whatever feelings I might encounter and be forced to face, but I just needed to see him. I didn't know what was or wasn't real right now, but after responding to him with such fear in our bedroom and then witnessing his mutilated body in my dream, I needed to see him happy. I needed to see us happy together before I lost those memories.

We had wasted so much of our time in our first years. We'd both admitted to that. Looking through these photos and reflecting on the four years since we left the city, I felt reassured that we'd lived a full life together.

He'd often accused me, rightly, of avoiding difficult decisions about our life. Or worse, I'd force him to make those decisions for us. Marriage, children, leaving the city—these were all conversations that would reach dead ends over and over as we treated time as a limitless resource.

We would never travel together again. We would never experience another adventure together. The idea of that was more than I could take. I decided it best to gather the pictures and put them away before what they truly meant dragged me to a place where I'd be unable to look at them ever again.

As I neatly piled them, a five-by-seven fell from the bunch. I recognized it immediately but hadn't realized that he'd had it printed. I understood why. He would have wanted it to exist in physical format for fear that it could be lost with a misplaced or stolen phone. Death terrified him. He'd shared this with me and told me that when he was a teenager, the very idea of it kept him awake at night. This photograph had given him faith where he needed it. I placed my hand on it and could almost feel the heat of that night, the sound of his voice as we walked through the dark streets of the old town, and the tidal wave of possibility that the image had seemed to unleash on him. Sometimes the very things that moved him deeply were those that deepened the distances between us.

2015

IT WAS OUR last night in Savannah, and we were making our way home through a wet heat unlike either of us had experienced before, both heavy with bourbon and sweat. As we passed the most recognized cemetery in the city, he lifted his phone and took several random shots into the darkness, jokingly saying that maybe he'd see something in them when he looked at them in the morning. His jest was for my sake—I knew that he hoped for this. He wouldn't openly say so, knowing that he might be subjected to the rolling of my eyes. He was a person who had little time for naivety or misguided hope, but he was spiritual in a way that he didn't often discuss.

Once or twice, we'd talked about our beliefs and the possibility of an afterlife. These weren't conversations I ever would have initiated, but I sensed their importance to him and did what I needed to see them through. He believed in something more, though he didn't subscribe to religion. Having grown up Catholic, I was well versed in the concept of the hereafter but held firm in my belief that when we were gone, we were simply gone. It upset him that there was no middle ground between us here. He'd sought my reassurance that I believed there'd be more to us after we left this life, but I could give him none.

The morning after taking the photos, he woke me at an ungodly hour. He was shaking my leg, unable to wait any longer to share with me what he believed he'd found. Through bleary eyes, I attempted to give him the attention he insisted this commanded and eventually just took the phone from him. The picture was dark but detailed and showed a small figure that appeared to be making its way through the cemetery, its head turned toward us. I wanted to deny it, but he had me and he knew it. I also knew that in the conversation that was coming, he'd expect far, far more than I was prepared to give him.

To start, he needed me to acknowledge that a figure existed in the photo. Reluctantly but quickly, I did. I was a man of logic and science, but there really was no reasonable explanation for what he was showing me, and I allowed him that. I would concede that I saw something, but that was as far as I'd go. He then made me look at the photos several more times, and I watched as they began to have a profound effect on him. The more he examined them, the more emotional he became. Once he'd exhausted himself, he looked at me, hopeful and awaiting a response. I looked back at him, trying to determine the best course of action. Ultimately, I fell short.

"We need to get moving," I said, climbing out of bed. "We want to get home at a decent time."

Later that morning we were several hours into the long drive home, and he'd been mostly silent for the duration. I knew he was angry, and I knew he was consumed, but I was choosing to let him work it out for himself and not say or do anything that could turn this into something it wasn't. I didn't judge him for his beliefs, nor had he ever judged me for my lack thereof. It turned out this was merely because we hadn't yet been put to the test.

"It was looking right at us," he finally said, solemnly. "You saw it. It was looking right at us."

I exhaled, not bothering to mask my dread. "Yes, I saw something. I don't know what it was, but honestly, baby, I'm not giving it much thought. I'm sorry. I just have nothing to offer this discussion."

He stared out the window at the Southern landscape whipping by us, not looking at me as he spoke. "You know the Bible. You remember it. I've heard you reference it more than once. You read it as a kid and absorbed it without question."

"This isn't that—"

"But you can't make room for this? You can't let yourself believe in the possibility that there's more to us than what we are, or that there's more than just what's in front of us?"

I gave him a moment of consideration. "I didn't carry the Bible with me through life," I said slowly, deliberately. "It was schooling, and I left it there. I believe in science; I believe in history. You know very well that I don't practise any faith. You're angry at me for not believing in something, but it isn't because I believe in something else."

Unlike in our traditional arguments, where he became emotional quickly, he was giving this time. This was important to him, and he was treading carefully.

"But did any of that stupid fairy tale resonate with you?" he asked. "Did you or do you find any comfort in it at all?"

I shook my head. "I'm not suggesting that you shouldn't take comfort in what you feel you see in those photos—"

"What we see."

"What we see. Regardless, it hasn't shaken my belief system. I never claimed to believe in nothing. Energy, things existing parallel to us ... I don't discount these possibilities, but do I believe you saw evidence of life after death? I'm sorry, my love, I do not."

He slumped in his seat. He hadn't looked at me once since we had gotten into the car.

"You're making me feel like an idiot," he said quietly. "I'm not crazy for believing in something."

"And I'd never suggest that you are," I said, glancing at him to let him know that I meant this. "If you take comfort in this, then you should allow yourself to do that."

He began to nervously play with his fingers. Despite my best efforts, we were in deep now.

"So if I died tomorrow, you believe I'd just be gone? We'd just cease to exist to each other? You can believe that two people belong together but that one day life and love will just be done with them?"

We'd been together long enough for me to know that this wasn't a childish fascination with a photograph. This wasn't the need to be proven right nor the need to have his beliefs validated. This was about us. He needed to find me in this conversation. If he couldn't, he'd be cast out into a lonely space where he felt as if the love he held for me was unrequited. I had lost him in this space more than once.

"I can't agree with you just for the sake of doing so," I said quietly. "But, sure, I believe that if there is something after life in this body, we'll be there together."

It was concise and it was simplistic, but I needed to patch this hole that was growing, and I needed to do it with some sincerity. I meant what I was saying, but this was as far as I could go.

He nodded, but his sadness filled the confines of the car. I inhaled it with each breath and felt the weight of it in my chest.

"I do," I continued. "If there is that possibility, then I have no doubt I'll find you there."

He looked down at his fingers. "OK," he mumbled, and then paused. "It doesn't make it all feel pointless to you, though?"

I glanced at him again and then looked back at the road. "What do you find pointless?" I asked, fearing where this was heading.

His face appeared worn, suddenly. He'd discovered hope, and I worried that I'd taken it from him.

"Everything," he said, staring at the highway ahead of us. "The idea that you can love with everything you have and one day it just turns to dust. Why put yourself through it? If you and I are just as meaningless as everything else, why do we do it?"

"You don't believe that," I said. "I don't believe for a moment that you find many things to be meaningless. I see you."

He finally looked at me, studied me for a moment, and then returned his gaze to the passenger-side window. "Maybe it's all just been a waste of my energy. Maybe if I cared less, I'd feel better. Maybe it's easier to believe there's nothing more and just give up."

We were alone in the car with another ten hours ahead of us. Had we been in the city or talking about this on the phone, I could have run. Here, I had no choice but to find my way through it with him. I hated it—not because he was challenging me, as he so often did, but because the spaces between who we were would reveal themselves, and there was little I could do to shorten them. A part of me wanted to be more like him, to believe in the unknown and find magic in the realm of possibility. That, however, wasn't me, and I didn't fault myself for that. Emotionally he asked too much of me, always, but the payoff was his love, and so time and time again I dug to find the words, the sentiment, or the touch that would let him know I was trying.

"Sweetheart," I said, removing one hand from the wheel and placing it on his thigh. "I love you now." I squeezed his leg gently. "I exist with you now. I don't spend time worrying about where that goes when we die because regardless of what we believe, what will be will be. Right?"

His fingers stroked mine as he stared down at our hands. "Maybe you just let go too easily," he said softly. "Maybe it's you ..."

With that, the conversation ended, and he didn't rebound for the remainder of the drive, speaking only when necessary.

We went to bed shortly after arriving home, both barely able to stay awake. The ache of the long journey, the bourbon of the evening prior, and the weight of his worry pulled the life from us both. I caressed his back as he lay on his stomach, his face turned away from me and his breathing slow.

"I love you," he said groggily, with sleep about to find him, I hoped.

"I love you too," I said, and kissed his shoulder.

He lifted his head, turned it toward me, and rested his cheek on his pillow, facing me. His face was tear-stained. He looked almost as though he'd been drugged into a trancelike state. This condition was familiar to me now. A deep depression had taken hold of him, and he wore it as though it had been beaten into him.

"I don't think death will stop me from doing that," he said, with eyes fighting to stay awake. "I love you and I'll be with you, always." He pulled his hand from under the sheet and touched my face. "It's okay that you don't believe that. I believe it for both of us."

I watched him as he began to drift, but I didn't speak. I hadn't known anyone like him. I'd never known anyone who could allow love to consume them the way he did. I became aroused but touched only his back. He was not okay.

"I'm sorry I am the way that I am," he whispered, a tear running down his cheek and onto the pillow.

I was about to protest, but he weakly placed a finger on my lips. "I think it's time for me to give up and try the medication again," he said, as his eyes closed.

I lay awake for the next hour, thankful that he was sleeping, and keeping watch over him in case he needed me.

February 2024

I STOOD OUTSIDE of our back door, my back pressed to the glass. The ground was snow covered, and the trees strained under the weight of what a series of storms had left behind. It was early evening, dark enough for me to be here without being seen by neighbours who no doubt would have felt compelled to try to speak to me. I had evaded their knocks this long, and the more time I spent isolated, the less I could stomach the idea of their conversation.

There were many things he'd disliked about owning a home, including the amount of space and responsibility, but our back-yard wasn't one of them. It had become our sanctuary. It was a place where we'd discovered a lot about ourselves. After years of living in the city, I realized I'd missed tending to a garden, and he'd found joy in the idea that he could successfully grow something from seed. On weekends he mowed our lawn and I saw to the weeds, and we both found this to be somewhat thera-peutic. We took pride in our space but ultimately didn't care how anyone else saw it. We needed only to be there together.

His favourite tree, a huge maple that stood to the right of the yard, loomed like death in these winter months. Its branches bare and its shadow cast over the snow, it waited as we did for spring and made no effort to disguise its misery. I stared at it now, remembering the days he'd lie beneath it listening to its leaves and sometimes letting his fingers roam the bark. In my thirteen years with him, I never saw him more at peace, and I'd catch myself attempting not to move or make a sound for fear it would remove him from where he was.

I scanned the quiet, cold yard. I was unsure why I was able to stand here at length. To look out the window where he'd stood every night, which overlooked this same space, would cause my breath to catch in my chest. Perhaps it was because we'd shared this perspective but what he saw and felt from that window was all his own. Missing him now was excruciating, but imagining the spring and summer ahead without him here sickened me. I wanted no part of it.

I backed into the house and slid the glass door closed in front of me. The cold had settled into me, and I caught myself shivering. With my hands on my arms, I noticed how small I felt. I barely ate, I didn't sleep well, and I did nothing to build or retain muscle mass. As I acknowledged this, my stomach responded accordingly, asking me to stop punishing myself and commit to keeping this body operational for at least the time being. I didn't want to. I didn't want to sit down at dinnertime and look across the table, only to not see him there. The thought of this made me angry. Where was he now? At my lowest, he'd appeared to me in our bedroom, but here I stood, yearning for him just as badly, and he was leaving me to do just that. If it had been real, why then and not now? Why then and not always? Why couldn't he be here with me, forcing me to eat and then putting me to bed? Why bother to do either if he wasn't here to push me?

"God damn you," I said angrily, staring out the glass into the darkened yard. "God damn you for leaving me here."

I turned my back to the door but stopped short when I noticed something blue flicker across the kitchen. I squinted my tired eyes and then felt a small sense of panic when I realized a burner on the gas stove was lit. The blue flame was burning high. I walked over to turn off the burner only to discover that the dial hadn't been turned, and was positioned as it should have been.

Obviously there's something wrong with the gas, I told myself. *I should have someone check on it.* But I couldn't see myself phoning a technician and inviting them into the house, so I dismissed the idea just as quickly. Everything was fine, the stove was fine, the fireplace was fine.

I stared at the blue flame and turned the dial several times. It burned strong. Wishing I could just run from the problem, I looked toward the back door. I wanted to go back outside and be in our place, but the cold had run through me, and I began to shiver uncontrollably. Though the fireplace had warmed me both times it had come on, had soothed me and provided respite from my self-inflicted suffering, I still refused to light it myself nor adjust the thermostat. I wouldn't get comfortable here. I'd be a traitor to even consider that this could feel like a home again, that it could feel safe.

I put my arms back around myself and decided to return to the wine cabinet. As I moved from the stove, a second burner came to life, and when it did, something gently shoved the left side of my body. Weak and fatigued, I stumbled and collided with the fridge. For a moment I stood stunned, wondering if the trifecta of sleep, stress, and malnourishment was sending me off balance. I straightened and slowly reached out to check the burner knobs once more. Before my fingers reached the stove, the two remaining burners came alive simultaneously, and invisible hands pushed me gently back against the fridge. I felt the imprint of them in my arm.

Instinctively I said, "Stop," and the sound of my voice caused me to freeze in place. I was aware of what insomnia and a lack of proper nourishment might do to a man, but this wasn't that. I fought not to allow this to swallow me. Motionless, I stared into the flames until my body finally found itself and I moved from the fridge.

I scanned the room, which was silent except for the hiss of the burners. I knew what I was doing. I was waiting for him to appear. The piece of me that had given way to that possibility surged to the forefront. I braced myself, rehearsing my reaction so as not to hurt him this time.

Both the cold and the strain on my nervous system caused me to begin to shake. A quiver at first, but becoming violent in only moments. The blue flames burned strong, and my eyes filled with tears.

"Please," I choked.

I needed help. Only for a moment, I needed help, desperately.

I found myself saying his name. I repeated it over and over, waiting for him to appear and fix this—the same way I waited in bed each night to feel his arm around me and to hear that everything was as it should be. The more I repeated his name, the more desperation crept into my voice. I couldn't stop. I called to him again and again until I finally screamed his name at the top of my lungs and then collapsed onto the floor. I sat with my back against the fridge and my head in my hands, sobbing.

The flames extinguished themselves then, and the house was silent. I stayed this way for some time before pulling myself from the floor, still shaking, and making my way up to our bedroom with weakened knees. I avoided looking toward his window and crawled into our bed, where I pulled the blankets up to my chin. I waited to feel him. I waited to hear the fireplace ignite, to hear the stove come to life. I waited for him to appear at his window. I waited for any one of these things to come and pull apart what was left of my sanity and allow me to completely succumb to him. Whatever it took to see him again, I'd sacrifice it.

At some point in the night, the smell of food being prepared in the kitchen made its way up and into the bedroom. Something probably hadn't been properly cleaned from the burners, and the flames had triggered the smell of it. He'd always been a chaotic cook. I didn't go and investigate. The smell was familiar. I felt at home again in a house that had come to be anything but. Before I could punish myself for that thought, I slipped into a deep sleep.

Three hours later I awoke and, without much thought, went downstairs and allowed myself to prepare breakfast. The heartache of sitting across from his place at the table made me cringe, but I also smiled. I smiled at the memory of the mornings I'd barely been able to keep up with his words as his train of thought derailed repeatedly. I'd sip my coffee, smile, and listen.

2015

It was Valentine's Day, and we'd talked about whether the day held any sentimental value for either of us. The consensus was that it didn't. With this in mind, I'd made dinner plans with a colleague and suggested we meet when I was finished. I hadn't seen him in several days due to work, and he'd insisted more than once that he needed space as he tried to adjust to being back on his antidepressants. The pills were wreaking havoc on him, but he believed that they could help, so he was prepared to see it through. I had misgivings but felt it wasn't my place to speak up on these matters. I had no life experience in this area and would simply support him as best I could. He had sound judgment for the most part; I would cautiously follow his lead.

We'd spoken before I left for dinner, and I knew then that something was amiss. He was angry but it was unfocused, and shortly before we hung up, I could hear his voice quiver. He told me not to worry about it, and as not worrying was something I excelled at when needed, I kept my plans, assuring myself that everything would be fine once I got to him a few short hours later.

When I arrived at his house that evening, I could sense that something inside wasn't right even before I knocked. It wasn't the usual unpredictability that preceded any time spent with him—I'd come to love that about him. It was quiet inside, and I could see little to no light through the windows. I knocked once and then turned the handle to let myself in, cautiously calling out his name as I stepped into his kitchen.

"You're here," I heard him say from the couch in the next room.

I relaxed my shoulders in relief and headed toward him, but as soon as I rounded the corner, an alarm went off inside of me. He was seated on the sofa, staring at the blank wall ahead of him, tears running down his face.

"Did you have a nice time?" he asked, still staring straight ahead.

He wasn't asking, and I knew that. His voice was unrecognizable, dark and hoarse, as though he'd been screaming.

"What's wrong?" I asked carefully, halting several feet from where he sat. "Why are you crying?"

"I'm always crying," he said, in a tone just above a whisper. "I'm always crying and so, when I cry, you don't notice anymore."

"What are you—"

"You left me here," he said, slowly turning his head toward me. "You called me at dinnertime, on Valentine's Day, to tell me you'd made plans. And then you left me here."

I was exasperated, but revealing that would ignite the situation, and the level of volatility here was more than I'd yet encountered with him. His face was as unrecognizable as his voice, and it froze me in place.

"I was under the impression that you had no issue with it," I said quietly. "We talked about it, at length. Yes?"

A sick grin crossed his face, and he stared directly at me, his tears still falling. Slowly, he pulled himself from the couch and walked toward me, unsteady. When he reached me, he put his hand on the back of my neck and pulled my face toward his until our noses touched. The smell of alcohol was evident.

"I want you," he whispered, his jaw so tight I felt my own teeth ache under the pressure, "to leave here, and never come back."

I tried to pull my head away, but he held firm.

"I want you to vanish, and I don't care if that means the earth has to open up and swallow you. I want you gone so far from me that I can never fucking find you again."

I was afraid—not because I thought he was going to harm me, but because I had no sense of how to navigate this. It felt as if there wasn't a word I could say nor a move I could make that wouldn't have sent this situation to the boiling point, so I pulled against his resistance just far enough for my eyes to meet his.

Calmy and softly I said, "I thought that you weren't supposed to drink while you were adjusting to these pills."

He released his grip on the back of my neck and slowly retracted his hand but didn't move. Our faces were only inches apart.

"And I thought ... you loved me," he said, with hatred in his voice, the grin having left his face. "I thought ... that you said ... you belonged with me."

I spoke his name, but before I could say anything more, he erupted and used my chest to push himself away from me.

"You're killing me!" he screamed. "You and I are fucking killing me!"

I remained calm and hoped that my eyes could plead with him. "What happened—"

"No!" he screamed, as he shoved my chest again, causing me to stumble back a step. "Take yourself and every fucking tear, and every fucking panic attack you've caused, and everything you've reduced me to, and pack it all up and get the fuck out of my life."

His chest was heaving, his eyes were wild, his fists were clenched. Until now I hadn't believed he'd turn violent, but I no longer knew what was or wasn't possible. I wasn't dealing with the man I'd come to know and love. His chemical imbalance had been exacerbated by the medication, vodka, no sleep, and—if I was being honest with myself—my decisions.

"I want you to listen to me," I said, severe and concerned.

"I am so tired of listening to you," he said, his sudden calm more terrifying than his outburst. "I'm tired. I'm tired, I'm tired, I'm tired, and I'd rather die than love like this."

"Can I please see the prescription?"

"I am not nothing," he said, a noticeable tremor running through his arms. "I am not nothing and I am not weak because I love you."

I exhaled, desperate. "Of course you're not, and I would never—"

"You don't know how to love anyone," he said, the horrid grin returning to his face. "You are so fucking empty I don't know how you stay standing." He grabbed the collar of my shirt, and his eyes burned into mine. "Get out of my life before you pull me down to where you are."

He released my shirt and we both fell silent, standing in a stalemate. His breath was still heavy, and his fists still clenched. I saw no sense in trying to speak to him but wasn't prepared to leave him either, not like this. I decided that my best recourse would be to find the prescription myself, so that I had the information at hand. He'd told me what he was taking many times but, true to form, I hadn't paid close enough attention to take note of the name or notice what he was going through as he had gradually increased the dosage.

I lowered my head, my gaze to the floor. "I'll go upstairs and get my things from your room, and I'll go."

I waited for a response, but none came. I looked up at him, but he was staring past me now, over my shoulder. His gaze had landed on nothing in particular, and his expression was now eerily blank. He'd drifted from me. I slowly turned and made my way to the staircase. It took everything I had not to look back to make sure he wasn't coming after me. He was unhinged, and I felt it best to avoid eye contact until he'd had some time without me in the room. Hopefully the storm would settle.

Upstairs, I was as stealth as I could be. I scanned his dresser, quietly opened his top drawer, and looked inside his nightstand. Finding nothing in his bedroom, I crept along the hallway to the bathroom and checked his medicine cabinet and the drawers under the sink. It was in the second drawer that I found what I was looking for. I carefully lifted the bottle so as not to rattle the pills. I rolled it in my hand, reading the label, and then pulled my phone from my blazer to quickly google the name of the medication.

As I typed, it occurred to me that I'd been upstairs for several minutes and in that time hadn't heard a sound from downstairs. He also hadn't come up to find me, and that was out of character. His need to know what I was doing and where I was extended equally as far as my need to smother him in every spare moment I had. He should have been wondering what was taking me this long.

I silently placed the bottle on the counter, left the bathroom, and made my way back down the hall to the stairs. I called his name from the top of the staircase, and got no response. Dread filled me as I moved down the stairs, mindful of what my gut was warning me I might encounter. I entered the living room, but he was no longer there. I quietly called his name and again got no response. Certainty hit me then, like a hammer to my stomach, and I ran down the three steps and into his kitchen. Something in me knew that if I waited one more minute to find him, it would be too late. I nearly fell down the last step but caught myself on the railing and spun around to find him sitting on the kitchen floor, his back against the cupboards and a knife in his right hand.

I said his name gently so as not to alarm him. "Please look at me."

He slowly raised his face. He was gaunt, and his eyes held no sign of him. "I am not nothing," he said, in a voice so battered, the words could have been his last. He raised the knife to his left wrist, and as I cried out his name and ran toward him, he dragged it slowly across his skin.

Two hours later we lay in his bed, ice rain pounding the window. What had followed was a blur: a brief struggle, blood, tears, and ultimately the realization that he hadn't cut himself so deeply that I'd need to call an ambulance. We had wrapped the wound tightly with supplies from his medicine cabinet, and once I felt the bleeding had been contained, I sat next to him and wrapped myself around his shaking body as he went into a mild state of shock. What he'd done had snapped him from his pill-and-alcohol-induced spiral, and with clarity he was able to quickly explain to me what he was taking, how much of it he was taking, and any and all other relevant information should we decide to get him to a hospital. We should have—of course we should have—but I believed I could handle it and that I had it under control. I still believed I was all he needed, even at this point. I stayed with him on the floor and held him until he finally asked if he could go to bed.

I helped him up the stairs to his room and, despite his asking me to leave him alone now, I climbed into his bed beside him. We lay there together, his head and his bandaged wrist on my chest. I held him close and played with his hair, which often calmed him on sleepless nights. He needed more than that now, but it was all that I could think to do. His breathing was shallow, and an occasional quiver ran through his lean frame. Otherwise, he was quiet. I wondered if he'd fallen asleep, so when he spoke, it was both alarming and reassuring.

"I can't take care of you like this," he said, his voice small and filled with shame.

I kissed the top of his head and held him tighter. "Maybe I just need to take better care of you."

He sighed a slow, quiet sigh. "You need to go," he said into my chest. "I'm not okay. I can't make you happy and I don't want to hurt you."

As was always the case, we viewed this incident from separate lenses. He felt this was the final break in our already questionable foundation; I felt it was time to repair the cracks. I pulled him to me so tightly that he let out an involuntary gasp: something I often did intentionally when hugging him.

"I think … that it might be time to reassess the medication," I said, cautious but committed.

Though I'd never push him, I felt it time to intervene. Inarguably, the medication wasn't helping him—it was destroying his already volatile ecosystem.

"And I also think," I continued slowly, "that it's time for you to let go and come and live with me."

He lifted his head and faced me. He was beaten and bruised inside, but I could see some semblance of himself back in those eyes.

"Why are you doing this to yourself?" he asked, appearing genuinely worried. "Why do you never hear me when I tell you that this isn't meant to be? Do you not want better for yourself than this?"

I kissed his forehead and placed my hand on his face, my thumb to his temple. "Because you're wrong," I said, holding his gaze. "I've never been more certain of anything in my life. You don't see it in yourself, but you take care of me in a way that no one ever has. I believe in you, and I believe in us, and nothing that has happened here has changed that."

And that was true, as it had been long before we'd even spoken. I'd never be able to explain it, but I knew it to be true. He fell asleep without responding, and I managed to stay awake long enough to ensure that he was resting peacefully.

One month later, he moved into my condo, bringing only his clothes, two barstools, and a plethora of shoes that took up residency in every available space in the closets. It was one of the first times in recent years that I believed life had purpose and that I was going somewhere. We were finally on a real path together, and this one had a future. Despite it all, that future looked endless.

February 2024

VALENTINE'S DAY HAD remained something that neither of us ever fully embraced. He felt it was a cruel day during which couples ultimately turned on each other when expectations fell short. His love existed in a place of rawness and devotion that neither money nor material gifts could touch. Though some years we made a dinner reservation or bought the other flowers, seeing him wake up on Valentine's Day, look at me through sleepy eyes, and tell me how much he loved me was more than anyone could have asked for.

And so it was surprising to wake up on this day with a special sort of heartache. We would have spent our day at work, then come home, worked out, made dinner, and gone to bed. That was our routine, but for some reason his absence today made me feel even more that I was missing out on him, on us. I wanted him here so that I could make every extravagant gesture I could think of, even the ones he'd hate or that would make him uncomfortable. I wanted him here so I could spend every waking moment of this day reminding him that he was mine and that he was my everything. The more I thought about it, the more guilt I felt over all those years we'd just silently agreed not to acknowledge the day. How could I have let pass any single opportunity to smother him and tell him that without him, my entire world would collapse?

I'd been feeling a little more like myself this past week, until today. I'd eaten one meal a day, sometimes more, and was busying myself with basic chores regardless of how unnecessary they were. I was letting myself sleep when sleep came to me, and though anyone on the outside would have questioned the state of my mental health, I believed that he was with me. I moved between this belief and the reminder that I wasn't, in fact, conditioned to make space for this possibility. Still, it gave me reason to keep going.

Today, however, it wasn't enough. I felt myself slipping back into the despair in which I knew I'd live out my remaining days. My attempt to uplift myself had failed, and I now felt foolish for having possessed such hope.

It was the wrong day to have answered the phone. I did so absentmindedly, without reminding myself how ill-equipped I was to manage these conversations. I was unsure how this person had even gotten my number, but the locals who had it must have shared it amongst one another for emergency purposes. The person was an acquaintance at best, and though before January I'd been known for my people skills, I could muster nothing for them.

They rattled on about their concern, how well they under-stood my pain, and how good it would be for me to get out and try to socialize a little. I stomached all of it in silence until they said his name. They said his name as though it were theirs to say and as though they had any right to speak it to me. In the moments that followed, I heard nothing but the blood thick-ening in my veins and a hum in my ears. I could have just hung up the phone, been polite. I could have just excused myself from the call and taken a deep breath, but instead I spoke— and what came out of me was vitriol so fuelled by sadness and rage that it knew no limits. It would have made him proud. I don't know how long it lasted, but when I stopped speaking, I collapsed onto the floor still holding the phone and was barely able to mutter, "Don't call here again," before I threw it across the room and watched it break into several pieces.

I waited for regret to come, but it didn't. I waited for the wave of shame to crash into me for the things I'd said and for, yet again, having childishly thrown an object at a wall as though doing so would bring me release. None of it came, and I sat shaking on the floor, full of hatred. I hated this day and every Valentine's Day before it. I hated myself and I hated him and I hated that any part of either of us had allowed even the smallest trace of complacency to enter our thirteen-year relationship. We were fire and rain, and should always have been. I wanted him here to fight with me. I wanted him here to push me to my limits. I wanted to pull on his threads just to watch him unravel, so that when we were finished with each other, we could put each other together again. We'd then make love in the way we always had, connected in a way I'd never experienced with anyone else. I wanted the pain of it all, knowing that at its core, it was a love so relentless that only we understood it.

I glanced at the clock. It was 6:00 p.m. Couples everywhere would be sitting down together to celebrate their love, and not one of them even knew what love was. We did—and only us. I had planned to eat dinner. A plate was sitting in the fridge, ready for me to reheat. Instead, I got off the floor, walked to the slowly diminishing wine stock, and grabbed a bottle. I'd sooner drink myself blind than see this night through.

Two hours later, I was where I wanted to be. I buried myself in the unrelenting mourning and the wine that made it okay to yield to it. I paced the house, glass in my hand, searching out the memories of us that would hurt the most. A photo, a film, a piece of furniture, food left in the cupboards. I decided on music and went back to his collection. I slid out the saddest album I could find—he had plenty of these—and moved like a vampire up the stairs to the main floor and through my lonely castle, waiting for the sound to fill the space and me.

The house was cold again. I'd allowed myself some reprieve this past week, as I knew he'd have wanted me to, but I'd decided not to heat it today. Chills ran through me despite the warmth of the wine, and I loved it. It was perfect. I was cold, weakened, delirious, and alone, and this was what I wanted—a complete free fall.

I walked with what stability I had into the living room and stood before the picture window, staring out at nothing in particular. It was snowing. Again. It seemed it hadn't stopped in weeks. It was stormy and cold and there were no signs of life. I wanted the snow never to stop and to bury me here under my memories of him. Spending this night together, just the two of us, staring into the storm like this, would have been every-thing to me. I envisioned the rare look of peace that would have settled over his beautiful face.

A familiar lump formed in my throat, and I thought I might cry. The tears didn't come. I just continued to stare into the storm in a slightly drunken haze. The bottle slipped from my hand and landed on the floor. Red wine spilled out slowly into a bloodlike puddle. I didn't move. I didn't feel it as it soaked the soles of my feet.

The wind picked up and its howl ran through the house, and with it came the familiar sound of the fireplace bringing itself to life. Feeling almost hypnotized, I turned to look into it and immediately felt its warmth on my face. I stared into the fire for several moments before the volume of his music began to rise from beneath me in the basement. The music quickly filled the house. It was nearly deafening, and it vibrated inside of me. It took me only until the lyrics began to understand why the song was awakening a sickness in my core, but also a sense of familiarity that closed around my chest like a vice. It was the song he'd tried to hum the morning he lay dying in the bloodstained snow, his finger caressing my face.

"My darling," I said with a breath, and then turned back toward the window.

Had I not been numbed by the wine, I would have startled. Instead, I froze in both fear and exultation at the sight of his reflection in the window. I'd been given no reason to fear him. The unease was pure instinct. He stood several feet behind me, motionless and looking toward me, but I couldn't make out his face. The wineglass fell slowly from my other hand and crashed to the floor, but I barely noticed. My eyes didn't leave him, and I took in every inch of his dark silhouette. His shoulders, his waist, his legs—every part of that body I'd claimed so many years ago and cherished ever since was near me again.

The music continued as though it was guiding him, and his bare feet began to take slow, seductive steps toward me. My breath caught and my heart pounded, but I wouldn't make a sound. Not this time. He wouldn't leave me this time. He stood directly behind me now. Tears ran down my cheeks and my breath quickened, but I remained still. He extended his left arm toward me. I used what willpower I had not to scream or turn to face him as his fingers reached my arm and his fingertips ran gently down my bicep and then slowly along my forearm. And I felt them. I knew him and I knew the effect of his touch, and this was him. Tears poured now from my eyes, but I remained still and silent, save for my breathing. His hand reached mine, and he slowly intertwined our fingers, clasped our hands together, and then, gently but firmly, pulled my body back against his. He slowly wrapped his right arm around my waist, holding me to him just tightly enough that I could escape had I wanted to, but enough force to remind me that I belonged to him. I'd expected his touch to be cold, but it wasn't. He was warm and he embodied comfort.

My knees buckled, and I struggled not to collapse. He tightened his hold on me and whispered in my ear, "Shh." The sound of him sliced through me, and I leaned my weight into his body. He slowly rested his left cheek against my right, holding our faces together. His every touch over thirteen years culminated in this space we shared, right now. Any love I'd felt in my life was here now as one force that had spent years preparing itself for this moment. I felt him in every part of me, inside and out.

For a moment I thought I was losing my balance, but then I realized he'd begun moving our bodies together. He swayed us to the music, keeping me wrapped tightly against him. We moved this way for the remainder of the song, and I closed my eyes, no longer feeling unsteady. He was guiding us. We were as close as we'd ever been, and his body against mine was home. His cheek against mine reminded me of every time we'd made love and he'd pulled my face or forehead to his. He was keeping us connected the way that only he knew how.

The music faded and his motions slowed, bringing our dance to a gradual halt. The room was silent, and I stood with him wrapped around me, my cheek still pressed firmly into his. I wouldn't move. I would stay here this way with him for eternity and never want for anything again. His love covered me whole, and his ownership of me filled me with a warmth I hadn't known since he had left.

My need to face him and look into his eyes became overwhelming. And so I began to turn my body, still pressed against his. Our faces remained in contact as I turned, my nose running against his cheekbone. I released my hand from his as I moved. I closed my eyes, preparing myself for a moment that I knew would once again change me and everything I'd ever believed. I opened them, but as I did, I felt the weight of his arms around me lighten, and could no longer feel his face touching mine. He was gone. The warmth of him lingered, and I could still feel him in the room, but his body was gone.

I held my gaze on the spot where he'd stood, waiting for him to return, but he didn't. My tear-filled eyes then roamed about the room but couldn't find him. I lowered myself to the floor and knelt in the spilled wine, feeling weightless and wondering if it was possible that I was dead. There was quiet, there was me, and there was the feeling that love had returned to me and that I had nothing to fear. I didn't feel cold, and I didn't feel alone.

2016

LIVING TOGETHER HAD proven to be a difficult adjustment for him. He feared me, and it took little more than my working late for him to second-guess his choice or find himself feeling alone in a home he didn't yet believe was his. Despite this, he took to domestic life as though it were his calling. He shopped and cooked for us, always ensuring that we were eating well. Not just well—if there wasn't a green on the plate, he'd have sooner thrown it from the balcony than allowed me to finish the meal. Our schedule became tightened by his need to control our time, which meant I was going to bed far earlier than I ever had in my adult life. However, this was the time that he allotted for lying in bed together and reading before sleep, and I loved this side of us. He'd rest his head on my chest and I'd play with his hair while we read, both attempting to turn our pages with only one free hand.

I loved it all. I adored the way he cared for me. I had family and I'd been in love before, but no one had devoted so much of themselves to making sure that I was my best self every day. Several months passed before I noticed him move about the space as though it was his own. He began to arrange things to his liking, and this period seemed to coincide with the gradual and final cessation of the medication. I watched his head clear, and though he still suffered with anxiety and depression, I no longer worried that he was going to harm himself. He was better here with me. I believed this wholeheartedly.

I took to this new life just as positively. Weekday afternoons, I'd catch myself counting down the hours until we were both through with work and could be together again. I'd coordinate with him and make my way to wherever he was en route so that I could walk him home. Waiting for him there would have been time wasted. I'd have missed those minutes of his chatter, during which he'd enlighten me with every minute detail of the hours we'd spent apart. Our walk home through the city streets became my favourite time of the day. The beautiful chaos of the city surrounded us, but all I could hear was him.

I'd settle into our nest on the twenty-fifth floor feeling as though everything had fallen into place. There were times I'd watch him prepare dinner and find myself so aroused at the very idea of him that I'd pull him away from his task, lead him to the bedroom, and ravage him. He'd oblige and would fully invest in our lovemaking—but he never failed to point out that I'd ruined our meal. He was everything to me, and we existed in that condo in a way that sometimes made it seem impossible that a world outside of it existed. Despite the differences between us, the heartbreaks, the uncertainty, and his looming fear that the bottom would one day drop out, we had made a home together.

That winter, I fell prey to a virus. We'd prided ourselves on having staved off the colds and flus that our peers and colleagues seemed to be so easily attracting, but illness had finally caught up to me, and I didn't recall ever having been so unwell in my life. It was my nature to push through these things and not allow work nor my fitness regimen to suffer. This changed, however, when I found myself in the presence of a natural-born caregiver. Place a wounded animal in front of him and he'd abandon all reason and devote himself entirely to its care. I was now that animal.

For two entire days he saw to it that I rested, ate properly, and had any and every movie I'd ever told him I enjoyed queued and at the ready. He checked my temperature hourly and scolded me if he caught me up for too long doing anything he deemed unnecessary. It was late the second night when I awoke in a sweat, my head throbbing and my body shaking involuntarily. He was, of course, awake beside me.

"You're getting worse," he said, placing a thermometer in my mouth. "I think you may need a doctor."

I scoffed and placed a hand on his arm to reassure him. "I'm fine," I said, with the thermometer between my teeth. "This is just running its course."

When he removed the thermometer, his eyes widened. "No, baby, you need a doctor," he said, fear creeping into his voice. "This isn't normal."

Gently rubbing his arm, I tried to smile. I wanted to keep him calm, but truth be told, the act of running my hand up and down his arm was requiring more strength than I had.

"Don't let your head get the better of you," I said. "This is a flu. I've seen you this sick before too. I'm fine—"

The immediate need to vomit took hold of me, and before I could say another word, I scrambled off the bed, stumbled to the bathroom, and crash-landed with my head in the toilet not a moment too soon. He was by my side in an instant with his hand on my back, soothing me with his voice. It was typical of his strength, this behaviour. At one moment he could be overcome with anxiety and the next he'd find himself harnessing it and directing it toward my needs. The worry he was feeling for me was being directed into my care.

He rubbed my back until I was finished, and helped me back to bed. I could see that he was scared and struggling not to insist that I seek help. Better judgment prevailed, and he allowed me to stay in bed instead of forcing me out into the cold to a hospital waiting room. Hours passed, and I worsened before levelling out. He refused to let me vomit in peace, and glued himself to me every moment because he knew I was in pain and couldn't stand the idea of closing the bathroom door on me. He had me choke down small amounts of water when I felt able to and managed to get some ibuprofen into me, which helped. Around 2:30 a.m. the nausea began to subside, and I lay in bed exhausted, still shaking. He lay beside me, holding a cool cloth to my forehead.

"What can I do?" he asked quietly. "Do you want some more water?"

I shook my head weakly and put a finger to his lips, my eyes closed.

"I'm going to be fine," I whispered, my head aching. "I just need to sleep."

He removed the cloth from my head, then reached over me and placed it on my nightstand. He snuggled himself onto his own pillow and pulled up the blankets to his chest. I thought that he was going to sleep, but I opened one eye to see him lying on his side, facing me, his eyes on mine. I couldn't help but smile.

"Go to sleep, you," I said.

"You first," he whispered, clearly as tired as I was.

"I'm not going to die, my love."

He shrugged. "We don't know that. That was pretty close … I almost tasted freedom."

I mustered a small laugh and put my hand to his chest to playfully try to push him away. He caught my hand and held it.

"Honestly," he said, kissing my hand. "Do you think you're okay?"

I pulled our clasped hands to my mouth and kissed his in return. "I have you, right?"

"Always," he whispered.

"Well then."

He studied me, our hands still entwined. "I like this side of you. When you don't make me work so hard for it. It's nice like this."

This hurt, that he still held against me every time I had and would still try to run from him. I couldn't ask him to understand why I needed him close and then would suddenly feel terrified by the very idea of him, something I'd never verbally admitted. I couldn't ask him to understand something about me that I didn't understand myself. I let go of his hand and placed mine on his face, but he gently took it and held it to his lips again.

"I hope you never get better and that I can keep you here, just like this."

I smiled again and felt myself drift off. I managed to tell him I loved him just before exhaustion finally put me down.

The following morning, he had me stationed on the couch while he prepared breakfast. He was quiet and seemed determined to let me rest, though I knew the silence must have been torturing him. When he did finally speak, what came out wasn't his usual disconnected flow of words.

"I don't want to lose you."

I raised an eyebrow and looked in his direction. "Why would you?"

Tears welled in his eyes. "You scared me last night. I haven't seen you like that before and it scared me. I don't want to lose you."

I reached an arm out and gestured for him to come to me. He put down the knife he was working with and came around the island toward the couch. He climbed onto it and then nestled himself into me tightly, pressing me against its edge.

I put my arm around him and kissed his head. "I'm much better today. Thank you for taking such good care of me."

"I didn't do enough," he said, his head on my shoulder. "It was probably my dinner that poisoned you."

"Shh. If you hadn't been here, I wouldn't have allowed myself to rest—and I would have been in far worse shape today. And no, your cooking didn't make me ill."

We were silent for a few moments, staring at the movie he'd put on for me, the volume low.

"I'll try harder next time," he said, in a quiet and menacing whisper.

I laughed through my lingering headache and gave him a small shake.

He looked up at me, his eyes pleading. "I don't want us to fight anymore. I want that to be behind us now. I just want to be with you."

I wanted to promise him that, that our life together could be easy and that we'd never hurt each other again. I kissed his head once more but said nothing. I knew us both too well, and I'd learned to let go of my daydream and to offer him the realism he respected.

"I'll never stop loving you, and you will forever belong to me," I finally offered. "I can promise you that."

March 2024

IN THE WEEKS following Valentine's Day, I pushed myself to take stock of what the house needed from me. I cleared out the fridge, leaving behind anything that wasn't yet spoiled, as it would remind me of his need to care for us. Everything found in the fridge and in the cupboards was part of a plan built on whatever he felt we needed more or less of at that time.

I shaved, I showered, I used product in my hair—not because I felt like myself again or because I thought it would make me feel better, but because I knew he was with me, and he could see me. He'd been watching me let myself go in every sense, and though I'd never in this life recover from the loss nor the details of how he'd gone, I could look like myself for him. I wasn't alone in our home. He was here with me now, and I didn't want a day to go by without him reminding me that he was still as attracted to me as he'd ever been.

I turned on the radio in the kitchen most days now. It was tuned to his favourite station, and it broke the silence that had held the house captive all these weeks. Periodically I'd have to turn it off, though, as all the small actions began to feel too familiar. I couldn't allow myself to slip into a place where I believed that our routine, our life in this house, was ever to be again. I'd catch myself humming along to a song he'd loved while I cleaned the kitchen counter and would then stop and force myself to replay in my mind the details of his death. I needed to make sure that I was grounded and would never stop mourning him. I was struggling to find the balance between the belief that he was here and the knowledge that he'd never truly be here again.

I hadn't seen him since that night, and he hadn't shown any other sign of himself. I didn't take this to mean that he was no longer with me, but I didn't know why he'd come to me when he had and why he wouldn't now. I also didn't try to understand it. This wasn't something that I had the mental capacity to make sense of. I just knew he was here, somewhere, and if there was any possibility that he'd show himself to me again, I wanted to feel ready.

For that reason, I was drinking less and forcing myself to bed at an early hour, as he would have wanted me to do. If I saw him again, I wanted to be awake to every single detail. I wouldn't show fear—wouldn't give him reason to believe he was unwelcome. I needed him to know that I wanted him here and wanted him to stay in whatever form I could have him.

I was in the bedroom, pulling together my laundry, when I looked over at his basket, still full. It couldn't stay this way. The smell of his running clothes was permeating the room, and the scent was turning rotten and no longer providing me comfort. I dropped my own clothes on the bed and walked toward his basket. *Don't think*, I told myself. *Just do what needs to be done.* Washing his clothing wouldn't erase him. I would fold it for him—something that had always irritated him—and put it away in his barely organized fashion.

When he first moved in with me, back in the city, I'd discovered unspoken details of his upbringing. He was self-taught in many things, including laundry. I'd once told him that he did his laundry like a college kid, and he'd responded by telling me I loved like one. That was the first and last time we ever discussed his home economics skills. If I so much as suggested throwing some of his clothing in the wash with mine, he'd remind me that he had his own methods and didn't need my help. I laughed every time, but I knew that there was likely something there: some pride he took in his defiance. He performed many tasks with a sort of reckless abandon. He'd figured out how to do them to get by but had never fine-tuned them. This didn't bother me. He was feral and I wouldn't have changed it. Watching him manoeuvre domestic life in his own way was an adventure.

I pulled his clothes from the basket, not wanting to admit to myself that I'd left them there that long and that the odour was now bordering on sickening. I felt ashamed; he didn't deserve this. I'd told myself it would hurt him if I removed any trace of him when what I should have been doing was showing him that I could still take care of him. I'd take care of his belongings and keep his space in this house intact and ready for him.

I caught myself then. I'd promised myself that I could choose to believe, but on the condition that I sustained a life lived without him. I stopped moving and allowed his clothes to fall from my arms to the floor. In an instant I saw myself from the outside and was no longer recognizable. The reality was that I was keeping house in the hope that he'd return to it. It was real—he hadn't been a vision. I'd felt him. The flames had also been real. I'd stared into them and felt their warmth. But none of this meant that we were now on a journey that ended with us resuming our life together. As I gazed at his clothing on the floor, I felt truly afraid of what I'd become.

For the first time in several weeks, I found myself forgetting to breathe and was suddenly forced to gasp for air. I'd had myself believing that I was on the mend and that I hadn't lost him entirely, that we could still find each other. I'd had myself believing that we could coexist in whatever way he'd allow. And now the sickness of it was crashing down around me, again. I was falling apart, and my inability to process my grief was causing me to develop coping mechanisms that I never could have foreseen. I could see it now, and I needed to stop.

I hated myself for thinking it, but I'd need to rebuild a life for myself inside of this house. I'd need to find ways to utilize my brain instead of letting it wander into the darkness.

I slowly picked up his clothing with the reluctance of a child who'd been asked to clean up their mess. My heart ached with every step downstairs to the washing machine. Why was letting go the only way forward? What if I simply didn't want to?

2017

"WHY DID YOU bring me here?" he asked, with barely controlled anger.

He stood against the window that ran floor to ceiling in our condo and overlooked midtown. His back was to the city night's skyline, and his eyes were on me.

"Why did you bring me into your home knowing goddamn well that you'd do this to me one day?"

I sat on the couch with my head in my hands, unable to face him. I wouldn't win this fight and had no right to try. Without speaking to him, without warning, I had pursued and accepted a new position that would require me to travel extensively for work. I'd be travelling internationally for weeks at a time, and given his own work and the structure of these trips, it wouldn't be possible for him to come with me. It had taken me days to find the courage to tell him, knowing what this would do to us and our life together—the life that had only just finally begun to establish a solid foundation.

"It isn't money," he said. "You didn't do this for money because we're fine, and you didn't do this for advancement because I've never heard you—"

"I was unhappy," I interjected, still unable to face him. "I've been unhappy with my work for some time, and there was an opportunity."

He tried to process it, but every new detail sent him further into the downward spiral I was about to lose him to.

"But I didn't know that, and that makes sense to you. Your partner of six years, whom you live with, had no idea that you were so unhappy in your job that you needed this desperately to get out. This is normal to you. This is what you think a relationship looks like."

"I should have spoken to you—"

"But you didn't!" he exploded. "You went through the entire process without speaking to me— No, fuck that, without even considering me!"

I looked up at him to assess how far gone we were. Should I try to explain myself, or should I remain silent and let him go through this in hopes that he'd find me on the other side?

"And then you come home, to our supposed home, and tell me you're getting on a plane tomorrow and I won't see you for a month? What the fuck is the matter with you? Who does this?"

"Can you come here, please?" I asked, reaching out a hand.

"Are you fucking kidding me? You're going to rub my shoulders until this is okay? Don't even think of putting your fucking hands on me."

Trying not to show signs of exasperation, I leaned back on the couch, my arms at my sides. What had I thought was going to happen? I'd had the ability to secure this job and all that would come with it, but I'd been unable to broach the subject with him because the conversation would inevitably become emotional.

He calmed, though there was nothing calm about him. "I didn't want to move in. You knew that."

I nodded. "I know."

"You pushed. And you insisted. And you painted this picture of what a life together would be like—"

"Isn't it?" I asked, my voice rising, feeling wounded by the insinuation that our life wasn't everything we'd wanted it to be.

He shook his head more out of frustration than in disagreement. "I am not a housewife, and I am not a work widow. I could have stayed who I was, and instead I'm this. You want every moment from me until you don't, and then you're gone without a trace. It's been this way, always. But this …"

I sighed. "I needed a change and I—"

"And you couldn't fucking talk to me about it. Instead of treating me as your equal, you treated me like a child or a fucking obstacle and removed me from the conversation."

We both fell silent. There was nothing I could say. I had taken the job, and I was leaving the following day. There was nothing more to it. Shortly after this trip, I'd be leaving again for the same duration. I had removed myself from our life without intending to, and he was taking the hit for it. I'd left him behind and, until now, I'd somehow not seen that.

"I never trusted you," he said, seeming resigned to what was happening. "I never trusted you, and it was never that I believed you were sleeping with someone else, or that you didn't love me. It was that I knew what you were capable of. Every time you shut that phone off or kept me waiting hours on end, I knew you were running and there was no way to bring you back."

I wanted him to stop, but there was no way I could tell him he'd been wrong to have had those feelings.

"I'm stuck here now, in your home."

"It's our home," I said, trying to find something salvageable in his eyes. "I'm not leaving you here, and it won't be like this always. This is for now."

"But you decided it, for both of us," he said, his voice beginning to shake. "You didn't wonder what my needs were—you just saw to your own. The most important thing to you is you, and you know what? That's smart. That's exactly how it should be." Tears filled his eyes. "But you should have left me the fuck out of it."

He walked away from the window and to the bedroom, where he pulled his overnight bag from the closet. I followed him against my better judgment and sat on the bed, deciding next steps.

"You're not leaving," I said.

He was already pulling clothes from his dresser. "I can afford a hotel for a couple of nights. From there I don't know. I won't stay here."

I reached out for his arm, but he pulled it away and moved on to the next drawer.

"I need you here."

He stopped what he was doing and glared at me. "Excuse me? Did you just tell me that you need me here?"

I didn't respond, and he continued.

"You need me here, but where the fuck are you?" he asked, before he resumed pulling items from his sock-and-underwear drawer. He moved toward the closet.

"I made a mistake," I said, looking at the floor. "I made a very big mistake and I'm sorry. It had nothing to do with you—"

His bag flew across the room and hit me in the chest. I recoiled, startled and wondering if he might be on the cusp of violence.

"It has everything to do with me!" he screamed. "You sucked what independence I had left from me and then you left me here for dead. I wasn't even a factor in your decision-making. Do you think I care about the job? I don't care about the job. I care about what you just did to us. You understand that it would be impossible to ever trust you again, yes? You understand that

I could never believe you when you lay out your intentions for me or when you talk about our future together. You understand that every step you took involving this decision was a deceit, and not only that, you didn't respect me enough to talk to me about it. What does that make me? What's left here?"

His volume made me sure that security would be at our door any moment. I needed to quiet him, but this seemed impossible. Everything he was saying was true, and every feeling he was having was valid. His chest heaved, and his hands shook. Panic was taking over, and I wanted so badly to help him but feared that if I tried to touch him, he might break and cause one or both of us physical harm. I expected him to surrender to it, which would force him to calm, but instead he lunged for his bag and yanked it from my lap, where it had landed. He put his arm through the strap and looked at me in a way that sank any hope I'd had that this was repairable. I'd never seen that expression in his eyes, and I realized I'd finally done it. I had lost him. If not all of him, at least a part of him that now seemed so far gone that I would never have it back.

"I love you," he said, with a strength I'd always known he possessed but that seemed to reveal itself only when he felt cornered. "All I want to do is love you, but you make it impossible."

"I know that," I said, "but I don't think this is cause for you to leave. We need to talk about—"

"Do you know what scares me the most about you?" he interrupted, not at all interested in hearing anything I could have to say. "It isn't the trust, and it isn't your ego or your arrogance. It's that you were so unhappy with such a huge aspect of your life and never told me anything about it. You were this unhappy and I didn't know."

I hoped for a moment we were turning a corner and would now be able to unpack this and find a way through.

"I didn't want to worry you or cause you any stress," I said. "I never want to add to your anxiety, and had I come home every day and unloaded this on you, that's what I feared I would have done."

He considered me for a few moments. "You could be unhappy with me, and I wouldn't know."

I looked at him in disbelief. "What? No. No, no, no, that isn't what this is. I am happy with you. I swear to you that isn't what's happening here."

"But I wouldn't know," he said, a challenge in his voice. "You lied to me without lying. You spoke to me every night about your day, yet I knew none of this was happening. You could be just as unhappy in your life with me, and you wouldn't tell me. I'm not waiting to see what happens then."

"Please. Don't leave like this."

"Why not?" he asked, tears streaming down his face. "I'm free. I can do anything and go anywhere I want—just not home. Because I don't fucking know where that is anymore."

He turned and left me then, not slamming the door and not screaming any last, venomous words. He left quietly, in a place of sound mind, and that scared me more than his leaving in a blind rage. I didn't go after him. Instead, I sat on the edge of the bed filled with a self-loathing that made me question every decision I'd made throughout our time together.

That night a severe thunderstorm ravaged the city. Rain flooded the streets, thunder rattled the windows, and I sat alone on our couch, watching the lightning. It was 3:00 a.m. He'd been gone seven hours now. I'd told myself he'd return in one.

He had places to stay; I was sure of it. He wasn't alone in the city, despite often believing that he was. He had few people around him, but those he kept close were of extreme importance to him. He could have called one of them if need be. I reminded myself of that whenever my mind wandered and I pictured him out in the rain, roaming the streets cold and alone.

I faltered and found myself picking up my phone to call him. At fault or not I'd never chased anyone, but the reality of losing him was sinking in. Though I wanted to wait and allow him to find his way back to me, for the first time I was unsure that he would.

But we needed one another, even at our worst.

I was about to dial his number when a sound at the condo door startled me. It was a key, though I hadn't locked the door behind him. I'd told myself that if he returned, I didn't want him to feel that I'd easily accepted his departure and locked myself down for the night. The door opened quietly, and I rose to meet him in the hallway. I moved slowly, afraid of what I might find. He was still wearing what he'd left in, and his ripped jeans and loose-fitting tank top were soaked through. His hair was matted to his face. He didn't look at me as he let his bag slide from his shoulder onto the floor. He said nothing as he dragged off his sneakers at the heels, using his opposite toes. He was shaking.

I said his name, but he didn't move. I took a step toward him, but he raised a hand. I couldn't just stand there and look at him in the state he was in, so I walked to the bathroom and pulled a towel from the linen closet before returning to him in the hallway. Without a word I held it out to him from a safe distance, but he didn't move, just stared at the floor.

I exhaled with both relief and fatigue, foolishly believing, as always, that things would now be okay simply because we were together. He raised a hand and slowly wiped the hair from his brow. Cold rain dripped from every inch of his body onto the floor. He opened his mouth to speak but then stopped.

"Baby," I said quietly, and he winced as though the word had sickened him. Despite this, I raised the towel in front of him. "Please," I said. "You're frozen."

He didn't move, and after a few moments I felt confident enough that he wasn't going to react violently to my touch. I positioned the towel around the back of his neck and wrapped it around his shoulders. It felt akin to discovering a wild animal on the side of the road and slowly, cautiously assuring it that you meant no harm and wanted to help. He let me guide him into the living room but stopped short of entering the bedroom. He pulled the towel from his shoulders, dropped it on the floor, and walked to the couch. As though every bone in his body ached, he lowered himself slowly onto it and curled up tightly.

"Please come to bed," I said, feeling I was desperately close to having him next to me.

He closed his eyes, and a shudder ran through him. "I'm sorry that I said it's impossible to love you," he said, his voice quiet and hoarse. "It's impossible not to love you, but I hate us both right now and I don't want to be next to you."

I watched him for a short while, wanting to hold him and wanting to keep trying but fearing him. He wasn't with me. He was somewhere else, and I didn't know what it would take to bring him back. I eventually retreated to the bedroom. The sun would be up soon.

This wasn't the last time he'd leave me this way. Over the next year he'd endure my absences, unanswered phone calls, and attempts to mend wounds when I returned. He'd do what he needed to do, and I knew that about him. He was loyal to a fault, but he became wild when tested. I didn't know where he'd gone that night nor where he went any night that following year when he disappeared from our place. I didn't know what he did while away, and I wouldn't ask. I'd let that torment me in exchange for keeping him because in the end, it didn't matter. He returned to me, and that was enough. He was where he belonged. He was with me.

After one trip, I returned home exhausted beyond measure. I was unable to leave our bed for an entire morning, and my body throbbed. Through his resentment he still cared—he couldn't change that about himself. He ensured I had water, forced me to eat breakfast, and went so far as to hold me briefly. I'd almost begun to feel secure with him again when he told me he'd always be there for me but that he'd never be able to save me from myself and wouldn't try anymore. It was clear to me then how much he blamed me for the distance that had grown between us. We existed now in a separate sort of togetherness.

March 2024

I HADN'T BEEN out for a run since that morning. The number of times one of us had gone for a run without the other in the last four years could be counted on one hand. Even so much as dressing for it would have made me miss him, and every single step along the way would have reminded me of him. I'd identify his anxiety triggers through the wooded portions of our route, as well as the areas where he'd stop his music to hear water flow. I'd find him everywhere, the way I found him in every corner of this house.

Today, however, I had a long conversation with myself about where I stood and where I was headed. Moment to moment I went from believing what I'd seen and felt to shaking my head free of any such impossible notion for fear of what it was doing to me. This morning, I felt a little stronger and had given myself permission to consider what my future might look like. It was gutting and I wanted nothing to do with it, but I asked myself again and again what the alternative was.

He had loved me so fiercely and promised never to leave my side, and though I'd never been able to put it into words the way he had, I had vowed the same. To move on in even the smallest ways would be like turning my back on him. Moving on was a betrayal. But if I stayed the course I was on, it would be the end of me, and he wouldn't want that either.

Sitting on the bench inside our front entrance, I laced up my runners. He'd sat on this very bench doing this very thing on our last morning together. I was sure I felt him next to me but tried not to become attached to the idea. The police had returned his running shoes to me, and I'd retied his laces and placed them at the door, ready for him. I'd been both shocked and relieved to discover that unlike every other article of clothing he'd worn that morning, they weren't bloodstained. I allowed myself a small smile as I acknowledged them now, remembering his refusal to ever properly remove them, an extension of his defiance when faced with the prospect of changing his habits.

My heart swelled and my smile grew. "Okay, babe," I whispered, still looking at his shoes. "Let's go."

Rather than avoid our route, I decided to face it head on. I was committing to at least trying to take care of myself; I wasn't trying to outrun him. I wanted to feel better, but I was as committed to carrying with me the pain of losing him. I hoped that I'd feel him next to me every step of our run. I could find room for both of us in this bid to move forward.

The first couple of kilometres were the most difficult. Everything about it felt wrong, and my body angrily rejected the attempt to simply pick up where I'd left off. My joints ached immediately, and it was clear what my period of abstinence from proper nutrition had cost me. I felt weak, I felt old, and I wanted to stop—I came close, before remembering the number of times we'd slowed for each other. I remembered the times he'd had panic attacks on this run and I'd walked with him for as long as he needed, patting his back until he felt calm and ready to try again. I remembered the mornings he'd fall back to wait for me when I was tired or inside my head, and how he'd pat my backside or run a hand down my spine to help me rally.

I forged on, and as the minutes passed, my muscle memory took pity on me and provided me just enough rebound to continue a little further. I knew where the route would lead me. I assumed I'd pass through this part of our run and feel nothing because I'd choose to feel nothing. Over the years I had repeatedly broken him with my ability to shut down and breeze through emotional catastrophe. I'd harness that ability this morning and use it to guide me through the place that had the potential to bring me to my knees.

I hadn't felt him with me thus far. I didn't know what I was expecting. Perhaps I'd believed that he'd find me because what I really wanted on this run was his companionship. It was possible my attempt to brace myself had been too effective and I was now feeling nothing other than physical discomfort, making it difficult to sense him.

I emerged from the college grounds and made my way down the road that would lead me directly to the pathway through the woods. My pace slowed as I approached, and uncertainty began to take hold. It wasn't a fear of the wolf: I had planned over many sleepless nights for what I would do if I encountered that fucker again. It was the uncertainty of what I would do to myself by crossing this threshold and revisiting the place he'd lay dying. What would happen when I came face-to-face with something that now existed only in nightmares?

The tree-lined trail loomed before me, and the untravelled snow was now creating resistance. I had every excuse to stop, but he would never have. If he was beside me now, he would have lead us through. My dream returned to me then, but rather than surrender to it, I bore down and kept moving, staring ahead and focusing on my legs as they began to fight the good fight. My heart did not ache, tears did not come, and my breath did not fail me. "Thank you," I whispered, and closed my eyes for just a moment in an effort to feel him next to me.

I struggled to lift my feet through the snow, but the further down the path I travelled, the more quickly I seemed to move. It didn't feel as though I was running away from something, but rather toward it. I grunted as I pushed myself forward despite the invisible weight trying to pull me backward and down. My breath became heavy, but the more I struggled, the harder I pushed through the snow and toward the place that I'd vowed never to pass again. I was maybe thirty metres away when the force that had driven me this far began to succumb to the limitations of my body. Slowing, I stumbled and scrambled to keep myself upright.

There was now only a small bend separating me from the spot where he'd been dragged from the trail. As soon as I rounded it, I'd be faced with a reality like none I'd ever permitted myself to be. I panted and winced through the pain now searing through my ankle, and I realized that I'd lied to myself. I was still lying to myself. I was no more aware of who I was or what I wanted than I had been two months ago. I knew full well that I'd set out on this path believing that if I visited the place where he'd died, I might get closer to him.

I should have stopped and turned back, but I continued to stagger through the snow. I was approaching the bend when I noticed a figure on the right-hand side of the trail. Had it not been for the dream weeks earlier, I would have collected myself and cleared the pained expression from my face, assuming it to be a fellow runner. But I knew who this was. I'd recognize his form anywhere and from any angle. It was him; it was my love, and it was not a dream. A part of me tried to fight it, but there was no battle to be won. He was here and there was no sense in pretending that this wasn't exactly what I'd hoped for.

He was still, and he was facing me. Light snow danced around his body as though he were orchestrating each flake. I watched him as I stumbled forward, driven by intent though unaware of what it was. I tried with futility to quicken my pace, moving with desperation—as though my survival depended on reaching him.

I called out his name, and then he began to move as well. One bare foot lifted from the snow, and then the other. He stepped toward me slowly and fluidly, and then broke into a gentle jog. I couldn't quite make out his face, but as he drew closer, I could see the blood. It covered his chest, his arms, and his midsection. His shirt clung to him. In this macabre and impossible moment, I found myself overcome with the need to feel his lean, strong frame under that bloodied shirt.

As he closed the distance between us, though, the violence of him startled me. I wasn't dreaming this time, and mounting uncertainty stopped me cold. He gained momentum and barrelled through the drifts as though they didn't exist. I could now see the severe expression on his face. His gaze, focused on me, seemed angry.

My desire for him quickly gave way to terror. I saw none of the love I'd felt from him weeks earlier. Instead, I felt unwelcome. He came toward me like a fierce animal, blood dripping from his throat, his right arm unmoving at his side. I closed my eyes. My breath caught in my throat.

"Stop," I said, terror barely allowing me to form the word.

I opened my eyes again to find him nearly on top of me, his eyes ice, a look of warning in them.

"Stop!" I screamed as I fell to my knees, placing my face in my hands.

I waited for the impact, but it never came. I stayed in my position, panting, face buried, for a few more seconds. When I lifted my head again, he stood directly in front of me, looking down upon me, his bloody wounds on full display.

His eyes were filled with tears now, and his pale face was filled with pain. "Stop," he pleaded, in a broken voice.

I shuddered and closed my eyes again, and when I reopened them, I was alone on the trail. Snow fell; wind blew. I waited for my breath to find me before gradually pulling myself up. I awaited his return, but he didn't come, and I was suddenly overcome with rage. I screamed his name twice and my voice filled the woods, my heart echoing off every branch. I waited and then screamed again but no words came out, just the sound of torment. I wanted to cry out for him once more, but my body wouldn't allow it. I collapsed back down to my knees in the snow.

2018

WE HAD DREAMS. Even in our worst of times, we had dreams of our future. We discussed what we wanted in the years to come, and where we saw ourselves in five to ten years. We disagreed on some things, but unexpectedly, we both saw ourselves in an endeavour that would have us working together. During afternoon beers on a Sunday or talks as we walked about the city on the weekend, we hashed out a daydream of one day owning a café. It made little sense, as neither of us had the experience or know-how, but we talked about it often. The more we talked about it, the more it took shape in our minds. We drew inspiration from our travels: "This flooring would look great in our shop"; "This is the kind of wine we'll serve"; "These are the type of chairs we'll have." We daydreamed so much that it became something that both inspired us and broke our hearts.

I was travelling less, but the damage had been done, and we'd never fully recovered. Though I could see him trying to find security in our life together, he never trusted me completely. He was also tiring of the city and feeling disdain for his day-to-day life. He believed there was more—better—somewhere else.

He had come to the city in search of stardom and found himself chasing that dream while forced into the confines of nine-to-five work. He'd found out the hard way that dreams didn't often come true. He was stronger than most, and he'd never expected anything to come easily, but it wasn't unreasonable to me that he'd reached a point of exhaustion. He took for granted the opportunities and experiences he'd had and was forever downplaying them to others, refusing to celebrate small successes. These things weren't enough.

I would have been happy with him anywhere. He'd never believe me when I said it, but home was where he was, even if he was smashing our glassware to subdue heartache. I could have closed my eyes, woken up anywhere, and felt completely at ease if he was next to me. So when he texted me in the middle of a workday to let me know that a café in his hometown had come up for sale, I didn't flinch. That night, we sat together on the couch in our condo, looking out at the city and pondering our future.

"This isn't where and it isn't when this was supposed to happen for us, but here it is," he said. "We've been talking about this more and more and now, suddenly, here it is. This doesn't have to be a daydream anymore."

I nodded, not prepared to object to the uncanny timing of it all. Days earlier, on a particularly gloomy Sunday, he'd asked me when we'd start to get serious about this venture and get out of the city, believing it was holding us back.

"I think we should take a drive up there, see what the situation is, and go from there," I said, knowing that one of us had to remain level-headed and open to the possibility that this might not, in fact, be a possibility.

"Do you want this?" he asked. "I mean the timing, the place. Do you see yourself doing this?"

He was genuinely concerned. He knew that I was guilty of agreeing to things that I believed would make him happy even if I wasn't truly invested. I'd do just about anything for him if he felt he or we needed it, and would rarely question his reasoning. This, however, was different. I could see the potential in this situation, as well as a viable solution to his discontentment in the city.

"I want to be where you are," I said. He began to protest, but I raised my hand and continued. "It doesn't bother me, the idea of moving there together. I'm as ready as you are to make a change for us. I've lived a good life here, but I never planned to stay indefinitely. I was always open to the idea of leaving."

He rolled his eyes. "You're so matter-of-fact about everything that it's impossible to know if you have any actual feelings about this." He paused. "What about your friends?" he asked, strained.

I wasn't sure if it was a result of the age difference, his possessiveness, or deeply rooted resentment over my behaviour on some of the evenings we had spent apart, but our respective social circles were mostly like oil and water. Our existence together didn't involve a great deal of crossover in terms of our friendships, save for one or two exceptions. I did, however, believe that he was concerned about the impact this move could have on me.

"They're settled," I replied. "Everyone is settled, and it's time for us to think about what that means for us. I'm more worried about you. You could leave your friends behind?"

He thought for a moment, and I could see a twinkle of anxiety in his eyes. He had certainly considered this, as he looked first to the worst case in every possible scenario. This would have been one of the first things that came to his mind after he found out about this opportunity.

"They would leave," he said, with conviction. "If they wanted or needed to, they'd leave me and not look back. I can't stay here for them knowing that if it came to it, I'd be the last man standing."

My heart ached for him. At times he could be so childlike and seemingly oblivious to responsibility or expectations associated with adult life. Then in a moment he could remind me of how battle-weary he was and how well he knew people. He knew the world around him, and he was painfully aware of what life could do.

I reached over and touched his hand. "You would never be alone. You would always have me."

He cocked his head, no doubt thinking about how alone he'd been over the last year, but then he looked me in my eyes and took a deep breath. "I think … this could help us," he said, pulling his hand from mine. "I don't think I can keep doing this here, you and me. I love you, but it's just gotten harder and harder, and I don't think we'll survive this if we stay here. Something has to change for me to believe there's a future for us—one that's more than the mess we've made here."

It was more than I'd expected, but he'd always had a way of expressing things with an intensity that left me feeling that unless I was prepared to emotionally match him, I pretty much had to concede.

I held his gaze and nodded. "Let's look into this. I think we owe it to ourselves to see if this is feasible, and if it is, we make it happen."

He studied my face. "You want this, though. This isn't for me. You want this for us and for yourself. Do you promise me that?"

I nodded again. "I do."

"Promise me," he insisted. "Do not do this for me because you'll end up miserable, and I don't want that for either of us. Think about this and promise me. It means leaving this life behind. All we'll have there is each other."

This warmed me, hearing him say that. In the midst of considering this rather ludicrous venture, he'd found a way to make it clear that what it boiled down to was the two of us.

He continued. "I've always told you that I'd prefer you in a little box where you'd be totally dependent on me to keep you alive. You could come out when I needed sex. Just for sex and then back in your box, where I could watch you and pet you and feed you treats because I know you like a treat."

I let out a small laugh as I said his name and covered my face with my hand. "Yes, you fucking lunatic, you've told me."

He pulled my hand away from my face and held my chin so I was forced to look at him. "This is that box," he said seriously. "Think about it. There's nowhere for you to run from me if we do this. Really think about this."

I put my hands on his chest, pushed him onto his back on the couch, and then climbed on top of him. I brushed the hair from his forehead as he laughed and tried to adjust himself under my weight.

"Oh my god," he said, in an exaggerated breath-deprived voice. "I hope your obesity doesn't follow us there."

This time, I took his face in my hand. "I am ready to stop running," I said. "I am ready for the life I've always seen for us, and I'm sorry that it's taken me so long to catch up to myself. I'm ready for you to cage me." I kissed him. "I'm ready."

We held each other's gazes for several moments before he kissed me and began to unbutton my shirt. Six months later, we would pack up our condo, mourn the life and the friendships we were leaving behind, and set out on this road together. Home was wherever he was.

March 2024

THE CAFÉ HAD sat empty for nearly two months. The very thought of opening its doors again sickened me, but it was bleeding money. He'd hate that I was allowing this to happen, but if I pretended that I was anything but buried under the loss of him, he'd hate that more. He had me in a perpetual catch-22, and as the weeks passed, I was more and more inclined to surrender to whatever I believed he would have wanted most.

The moment in time where I'd believed I could move forward and survive, though never be happy, was gone. Memories of us haunted me every waking hour, and had placed me right back where I knew I'd always remain: devoted to my grief, confused, and swallowed by rage and the brutality of a life without him. I didn't understand what was happening to me, to us. He'd asked me to stop, but I didn't know what. He'd also ensured that I'd never set foot on that trail again, though I didn't know if that had been his intention. The sight of him that morning, tears in his eyes and bleeding before me, it was a close second in its cruelty to the memory of his last breaths as he lay beneath me.

A week after my encounter with him in the woods, I decided it was time to return to the café. It was near midnight; the town was dark and the streets silent as I entered through the back door. The moment I was inside, my stomach turned. The memories of our journey to this place, our efforts in building it into the success it had been, our time together here each day—they all came thundering down on me. After disarming the alarm, I stared down the long hallway leading to the main room, half expecting to see him waiting for me. He wasn't. The hum of the fridges was the only sound, and everything appeared exactly as we'd left it on our last working day together in early January. A part of me had hoped I'd find it in shambles due to a burst pipe or small fire, which was foolish, as I would have been notified. I had hoped to find it in a state that would allow me to turn my back on it and never return.

I took a deep breath, exhaled, and walked down the hallway to the service bar. It was there that I found him. He was standing behind it with a kind smile on his face. I froze in place and swallowed, doing my best to assess his state. I should have been afraid, but he'd never tried to harm me, and the regularity of his visits was conditioning me to expect that I could see him any time, any place. He lowered his head slightly and looked at me in a way that suggested he wanted me to listen.

"You and me," he said, his tone comforting and calm.

He had spoken to me this way many times, more so in recent years as our roles changed and I became increasingly reliant on him to guide us. My heart beat so loudly that I was unsure if my words would be heard over its thud, and it took everything I had to release them from my trembling mouth.

"I need you," I said, choking back tears. "I need you to come home."

His smile faded, and he reached for me across the bar. I hesitated only a moment before raising my hand to meet his. Adrenaline ran through me. I was going to feel him again. I held my breath as our hands drew close, denying my fear and its insistence that I withdraw. Our fingers connected, and he intertwined his with mine. His touch was real. It was him in his entirety, and I was again stunned by how warm he felt. I began to sob.

"Please," I said, as I looked into his eyes. "Please come home."

I could barely see through my tears, but he held my gaze. He was sharing my pain. He looked at me the way he always had when he believed I was suffering. He didn't speak, but I could see by his expression that he felt helpless. Whatever I was asking of him, we both knew it wasn't possible, and my pleading was hurting him.

"I need you," I said, ignoring the voice inside of me begging me to stop for both our sakes. "Don't leave me here without you. Please. Please."

I let go of his hand and collapsed on top of the bar, my face in my folded arms. My body heaved as sobs took control of me. I knew when I looked up, he'd be gone. I knew it and I couldn't bear it and so I kept my head down until my tears had run dry.

When I returned home a short while later, I went straight to our bed and climbed under the covers. I lay on my side and pulled his pillow close to my face. I stared toward his window, not waiting for him and not wondering if he'd come. I just stared, numb.

"You and me," I whispered.

2020

We sat on our couch in front of the picture window, sipping coffee and staring into the rain. The pandemic had arrived in Ontario at nearly the very moment we arrived in our old new town. With the café forced to close just days before our grand opening, and the world at a standstill, we had nowhere to be but here, in our new home. It was a dream for me, though I knew he was scared—not of the virus but of the uncertainty of everything. Our final attempt to find stability in a life together had been quickly turned on its head.

We'd made the most of the time so far. We'd unpacked our boxes and painted a couple of rooms. We made love every day and rang in cocktail hour promptly at 5:00 p.m. On warmer days, we stood in front of the gardens we'd acquired and he'd devise his ill-conceived plans for the spring, though it was clear he had no idea what he was embarking on. We'd both grown up in small towns, but he was a city kid at heart. He would need my guidance, but I also couldn't wait to see him tackle these projects with characteristic recklessness.

We'd purchased bicycles and sometimes went on long rides through town. It was on one of these rides that we discovered the trail we'd come to adopt as part of our run. Allowing him to ride ahead of me, I'd watch as the sun caught him from between the trees. We'd sometimes dismount and just take in our surroundings. Despite the difficulty of what we now faced, we felt lucky. On one afternoon ride, he looked at me with an expression that suggested he was about to share something truly intimate.

"One day we're going to fuck in these woods," he said.

I shook my head and laughed, then picked up speed to ride ahead of him. He was what he was.

During these weeks I found myself speaking to him more easily than I ever had. I shared with him when I was frustrated with the house or when I had misgivings about his ideas for the café. I told him when I was feeling homesick for our former life, and I let him reassure me when he saw me show any small sign of struggle. I didn't know what it was about being in this new place that made me so much more open to him, but we'd never been closer.

Taking another sip of coffee, I extended my leg and tapped his with my foot. He looked down at it and then up at me, smiling.

"Yeah?" he asked.

I gestured for him to move closer on the couch. "What are you doing all the way over there?"

"I thought maybe you needed some space. This is as much as I could bring myself to give you. I considered going to another room but ... no."

I grinned, thankful that this side of him hadn't changed in our ten years together. His possessiveness hadn't faded, and I hoped it never would.

"Well, I'm pretty lonely over here," I said. Thinking this might evolve into sex, I placed my mug on the floor.

"Well," he said, glancing at me and then looking toward the window, "clearly you have some dependency issues, and that's something you should work on. I mean, at some point I'll leave to shower and what the fuck are you gonna do then?"

I laughed and kicked at him with my foot, but he moved his leg in time to evade me. He smiled but didn't turn from the window. He was pensive, and I knew he was thinking about more than the rain.

"Are we going to be okay?" he asked.

"What do you mean?"

"I mean do you think this will pass and we'll be able to salvage the shop and make a life here? Or did this move just fucking kill us?"

In the first days of lockdown, he'd seemed unaffected. The pandemic was just something that was happening, and with enough going on to occupy his mind, he was uncharacteristically neutral about it all. He'd also seen it coming—he'd been watching the news in the weeks prior to leaving the city. He wasn't afraid, but it angered him that no one had foreseen the inevitable. I crawled over and wrapped my arms around him, but he was tense and remained focused on the view outside.

"I mean it," he said. "There's a worst-case scenario here."

"No, there isn't. Whatever it takes, we'll make this happen. You'll make this happen."

He looked at me with annoyance. He didn't have to speak his mind. I'd held on to my job and was able to work remotely on the expectation that I'd periodically return to the city. Fortunately, the lockdown had ensured this wasn't a bridge we'd have to cross anytime soon. This was to be a fresh start. The job coming with us here was a stain, and I knew that.

He softened, seeming to take comfort in my reassurance now. He reached his hand and ran the back of his index finger down my cheek. "Thank you," he said. "Thank you for everything it took to get us here, to make this move."

I clasped his hand in mine. "We did it together. This is us, babe. You and me. We're going to do this."

He squeezed my hand briefly and then kissed my fingers before returning his gaze to the window. "I know," he said softly. "I believe in us."

I fought through his tension and pulled him as close to me as I could manage. After a moment's resistance, he placed his mug on the floor and folded into me.

"Let's say everything works out," he said, as we both stared out of the window of our new home. "We build this place up and create a life here in this town."

"Yes?"

He paused for a moment. "Well, what next? What comes after that?"

I sighed and smiled, kissing the side of his head. "Can we just get through this part first?"

"Yes, of course," he said quickly, having the self-awareness to know that he was getting far too ahead of us. "But where do you see us five years from now? We aren't getting any younger, and it's been just you and me for a long time. Don't you feel like we're getting to the part where we're supposed to have procreated, or at least be talking about it? I mean, it isn't for lack of trying, but clearly I'm barren."

I tensed, knowing where this was heading, but I appreciated the humour to help ease us in. We'd actually discussed the idea of children many times, and each time we'd ultimately decided that neither of us felt equipped to see it through. It could have been his approaching midlife causing these feelings to resurface, or the increasing awareness of time as it related to our age gap, or something as simple as witnessing more of his peers get married and adopt children. He needed my patience now, and more than anything, he needed me to reaffirm my commitment to the life we'd chosen.

"I thought we agreed that you and I were enough," I said. "That neither of us truly wanted to go down that road."

"I know that. And we are enough. But being in this house … it's big for the two of us and it feels empty, no? It was meant for a family."

I pulled away only enough to face him. "It was meant for us. It doesn't need anyone but us. But if this is something you need to talk about again, then we should talk about it."

He was silent for a short while, then shook his head as though waking himself from a dream. "Forget it. I can barely take care of myself half the time. I don't know why I keep bringing it up."

"Darling," I said, brushing his hair from his forehead. "You'd make an amazing father, and if you still feel you may want that, you need to tell me. But for what it's worth, I believe in us as we are, and I'm happy with our life. I'm happy with where we are and where we're heading. I need nothing more than you."

He offered me another smile and then returned his gaze to the window. "It's just … time," he said solemnly. "I wouldn't trade you for anything—I'd give my life for yours and you know that." He turned to me with his brand of almost violent sincerity before softening again. "But I'm scared that we missed something somewhere in these years and maybe it's too late to get it back."

"There are other things," I said, deciding this warranted my going all in. "There are other milestones that we don't have to miss out on simply because of our age. We haven't discussed marriage in some time …"

He winced. "Don't be gross. There's no need for that."

I smiled and shook my head. I needed to get to the heart of this and find out what I could possibly do to put his mind at ease. "Hey." I said his name softly. "We're going to be very happy. I believe that."

He just smiled politely and looked away. I watched as the weight of his thoughts settled on his shoulders. I believed the words I'd spoken, but I couldn't have predicted that this part of our journey together would ultimately signal our end, nor could I have predicted the mountain of regret that would be left behind.

April 2024

I'D MADE IT to April. It had officially been four years since we relocated to start our new life together. Over the last three months I'd caught myself wondering what would have become of us had we never left the city. Would he still be with me? Or would the marks on us have taken their toll despite our love for each other? Though I didn't believe that either of us would ever have truly given up, I found some reassurance in the possibility that maybe losing him hadn't been preventable.

Had he walked out the door and vowed never to look back, I wouldn't have recovered from the loss. Knowing he was alive and existing somewhere could have carried me, though. The possibility that he might one day come back to me would have given me hope. I had that hope now, but the light that kept it alive was costing me everything. Every day I moved between knowing that I needed to move on and believing that I could coexist with him here always. That his visits could sustain us. I was still living for him, and each time I told myself that I could let him go, that I could stop pleading for him to return, I knew I was lying to myself.

An unexpected early thaw had seen the snow fade from our lawn in a prolonged and ugly farewell. More dead grass and mud than flowers and sunshine—that was the reality of spring.

Neither of us had ever cared for this period, but seeing the way a mild afternoon affected him had always reminded me of what was to come. He had embraced every season, had found ways for us to make the most of the cold and rain, but he radiated come summer.

Standing in the kitchen, I stared into the backyard at the gardens that awaited my care. I wanted nothing to do with them. Instead, I wanted to put my fists through the window. I'd never again look out and see him soaked in sun, his hair tousled by a breeze. I'd never again see him stoned by the summer air. How was I going to fill these months when every waking moment spent in this yard had been spent with him? Not to mention the upkeep. I'd proudly become the sole owner of that house on the block—the one at which passersby would shake their heads in disapproval. Good. Fuck them.

After seeing him at the shop, I'd returned to the house and not left since. Each time I saw him, I found it more difficult to pull myself together afterward. I'd slide back into this condition of staring out of windows, evading sleep, barely eating, and wondering if I'd turn a corner and find him there.

I was angry at him for doing this to me, but more angered by the idea of him never returning. It was a constant struggle and of course, I couldn't speak to anyone about it. There wasn't a soul on earth I trusted enough to disclose this to. I was alone with him here, and though I tried not to admit this to myself, this was the way we'd always preferred it, and the way it had always been. Just the two of us.

I placed a finger on the kitchen window and slowly let it run down the pane before dropping my hand to my side. Maybe taking care of the yard would give me purpose and comfort. It was possible that adopting the tasks he'd taken such pride in would bring me closer to him. It was a nice thought, but imagining it made my stomach clench. I feared that I'd only miss him more.

"What do I do?" I whispered, tempting him to return and hold me again. "What do I do here without you now?"

My gaze became a daydream, and I sank into the memory of him stepping through the pumpkin vines the previous summer. They'd taken over a full quarter of the yard and patio. He would do this each day, count the pumpkins and gently pull aside the giant leaves in hopes of discovering new growth. His knees would be grass stained from his turning of the fruits to ensure they didn't flatten on one side. He'd forget to do this more often than not and would end up annoyed by the result but nonetheless filled with the magic of having grown them.

He had worried I'd protest his growing them for fear of what they'd do to the grass. Before meeting him, I never would have allowed something so unruly to run amok across a garden or otherwise well-landscaped yard, but I'd come to see things differently through his eyes. Together we found the joy in things that others would find trivial. Watching these vines begin their growth early in the summer and then weave their way into our lives as the months passed was something that made this space even more exclusive to us. No one else could ever have shared or understood it.

I swallowed the familiar lump in my throat and stepped away from the window. What would we be doing on a grey Sunday such as this one? He would want us to keep busy, but there'd be moments of quiet when he'd allow me to rest and possibly even let me convince him to join me. I poured myself more coffee and went to the living room, where I took my seat on the couch in front of the picture window.

I closed my eyes to imagine him next to me staring out at the melancholy April afternoon. I could almost feel the weight of him, could almost hear him insisting that if I loved him, I'd need no more space than this. I smiled and hoped that when I opened my eyes, I'd find him there.

2021

"Do you think about it at all, though?" he asked, his head hung low, as though he could barely bring himself to face the conversation.

"Having kids?" I asked, bracing myself for whatever might come. "You know I do. We've discussed this many, many times. But I know who I am and what I want—and don't want—at my age."

"No. I've discussed it. You usually just wait until I've finished and then change the subject."

I exhaled and placed my hands on the kitchen counter. "Yes, of course I think about it. I have a lot of guilt where this is concerned. You clearly have regret, and I'm the one that held you back from something that you might have otherwise pursued."

He looked surprised, and I couldn't blame him. We were constantly adjusting to the new us here, and sometimes it seemed we were only just beginning to become truly acquainted. He wasn't accustomed to my admitting such feelings, let alone seeming open to a conversation such as this. I was not, in fact, open to the conversation and would have preferred to hide from it. But more than once he'd reminded me that life was short and the years between us were only going to present more challenges as we carried on down our path together.

"I don't want that," he said, his eyes on mine now. "I don't want you to feel guilty about decisions we made together. We both let this go, but I just can't help feeling like ... like I'm not sure we should have."

I held his gaze, the weight of what must be going through his mind sitting heavily on my own chest now. Though I had regrets, I didn't consider children to be a possibility at this point, and that was my burden to bear. What was killing me, though, was that he still had time—and the realities of that time and our limitations due to age were crashing down on him.

"I know what you must be thinking when I bring this up," he said.

I was unsure whether he was waiting for me to solve that puzzle, but I chose to remain silent.

"The anxiety, the years of pills and drinking, a cut wrist ... who the fuck am I to think I could raise a kid?" he said, looking at the floor again.

I shook my head and moved around the counter to him. Grabbing his arms, I pulled him away from his breakfast preparation and turned him to face me.

"No," I said sternly. "I don't think those things. I think you'd make a great father, and I know that what you're going through right now must be very difficult." I exhaled. "I feel very much to blame for the position you're in now."

He pulled his arms free but only so that he could wrap them around my neck. I buried my face in his shoulder as he caressed the back of my head.

"I'm sorry," he said. "It's just me. This is hard. Getting older and living with these choices is hard. I know we made the right one for us, I just ... It's hard." He moved his head back and looked at me. "But we made this decision together, and I wouldn't trade us for anything. Ever. I've told you that." He placed his hands on either side of my face. "Do you hear me?"

I nodded.

"I don't mean to upset you when I bring this up, but it scares me," he continued. "I'm scared. Are you not?"

I sighed and pulled his hands from my face to take them in mine. "It doesn't scare me, because I have you. We have each other, and I'm happy with that. I really am. It is, truthfully, all I need."

The worry that filled his face was immense, and I knew I had no words that would convince him no mistakes had been made. We had both admitted that we'd wasted our early years together on childishness, on the hunt and the chase, and it was something we both regretted greatly. This conversation was the cost of that time.

He kissed my cheek and ran his thumb across it. He managed a small smile and took a deep breath, a sure sign that his anxiety was posing only a minor threat. Still, we'd need to tread carefully. One more deep breath and a roll of his shoulders and he seemed to settle just slightly. Enough that we could continue.

"You know I've got you, right?" he asked. "You know that whatever may come and no matter how hard it gets, I've got you."

Smiling would have made light of the conversation, but his words did warm me. I kissed him softly. "I know that," I said, and pressed my forehead to his, moving it gently back and forth. "I've always known that."

He kissed me then, more firmly, as he did when he wanted me to know that he meant it—an embrace of purpose more so than affection.

"We have a beautiful life together," he said. "I know that. Please don't think I'm ungrateful and please don't ever, ever think that I blame you for our decisions, because I don't. I know at our worst I said otherwise, but I never meant it. I just wanted to hurt you. I wish we could have time back. I wish it so badly. But we can't, and I just need you to promise me that we're going to make the most of this life together. If we don't fill this house and this life with kids, then we have to fill it with everything else we need for us to be happy." He tilted my head up by my chin. "Promise me that. We make these choices worth it."

I couldn't quite rebound from the feeling that I'd failed him, but I nodded slowly. "I promise. I love you, and I will adore every year we have together and never look back."

He kissed me again and then pulled me into his body, slowly rubbing my back. He was comforting me at a time when he needed it far more than I did.

"You belong to me," he whispered in my ear. "You belong to me and I belong to you and don't you forget that because at the end of the day, it's all that has ever mattered."

Despite the discomfort of the conversation and the many questions left hanging in the air surrounding us, I became aroused by his possessiveness. Throughout the years of running from him, all I'd ever really wanted was to belong to him, to submit to him.

Whatever shape our life took, I would be his to my last breath.

April 2024

A SPRING STORM was sweeping through the town. The windows rattled under the severity of the thunder. We would have sat at the window, taking in every strike of lightning, but tonight, I felt unnerved. The sound of the wind putting strain on the branches out back put me on edge. I tried to keep busy, feeling pathetic for allowing a thunderstorm to leave me so uneasy. This was out of character, but these days I had no idea who I was or wasn't.

I resisted the urge to call a friend or family member to help pass the time, knowing what would happen. The storm would pass, and I'd then find myself in the depths of a conversation I couldn't escape and hadn't, in fact, wanted to have. There remained no one out there who could understand what was happening to me or help me through feelings that couldn't be described nor explained.

I decided to go downstairs to turn on the television. Just as I took the first step down to the basement, the doorbell rang. I froze, unsure that I'd actually heard it. Was the wind playing tricks on me? The longer I remained in place, the more the hairs on my arms began to rise. After about fifteen seconds the doorbell sounded again, and I jumped as though it had been a gunshot.

It had to be a mistake. No one tried to visit me anymore, and in this weather and at this hour on a Saturday evening, it wouldn't be a marketer of any sort. I considered ignoring it and carrying on downstairs, but given I was only halfway through the doorway to the basement, there was a good chance that whoever it was could see me through the stained glass on the front door. Plus, there'd be no way I could relax wondering if someone was or had been outside the house.

I gave my head a shake, reminded myself of who I was at my core, pulled myself off the step, and moved toward the door. I had nothing to be afraid of, and if it happened to be a friend or member of his family, I wouldn't leave them standing in the rain. Or I would and just tell them to fuck off. *Grow up*, I told myself, as I turned the knob and pulled open the door without allowing myself time to hesitate.

On the doorstep, drenched, his hair matted to his forehead, was an acquaintance we'd made not long after arriving in town—a handsome man in his thirties whom we saw mostly at the shop but had spent time with socially once or twice. He looked afraid and embarrassed and apologized before I could say hello.

"I don't know what I was thinking," he said, rain falling from his lips. "I should have called or stopped by weeks ago but I didn't know what to say and so I talked myself out of it and then time just kept movin' on and the longer I waited the harder it got and I just … I'm sorry. I'm real sorry."

I stared at him dumbfounded, wondering what on earth had possessed him to do this now. As angry as I was perplexed, I found just enough decency in myself to cut through the haze and tell him to step inside out of the rain. He protested initially, but a huge clap of thunder nudged him indoors. He closed the door, bringing with him a silence that filled me with dread. Now we were two people in a room and would have to speak to each other. There'd been no one inside this house since he died, and now there was, and it felt impossible.

"So …" I said, looking at him as though he were an alien.

"I am so sorry for this," he said, his breath smelling faintly of whisky. "I was driving home and saw a light on and thought to myself, I should just do it now, y'know? Before I talk myself out of it again."

"There was no need," I said, folding my arms, realizing the whisky he'd downed would have been what guided him here. "It hadn't even crossed my mind."

I felt the sting in my words, knowing that they implied this person hadn't even crossed my mind, but that was also true, so I decided I needn't bother to redeem myself.

"I appreciate you stopping by," I said flatly, "but it was unnecessary for you to feel guilty."

He nodded, and I noticed he was shivering. Of course he was. The evening was cool, and he was soaking wet. I found myself in the dilemma of whether to offer him a towel and invite him further inside or just get rid of him as soon as possible. I wanted him gone. This was already more time than I'd spent face-to-face with another person since the funeral, and it wasn't feeling any less excruciating than it had then. He lifted the peak of his ballcap and wiped his forehead.

"This was rude of me," he said, in his small-town twang. "I'm being rude. I'm real sorry, I just wanted to let you know that I always thought he was a really great—"

"No," I snapped, holding up my hand and shaking my head. "No."

His eyes widened, and I could see he was unsure of what he'd done.

"Don't do that," I continued. "You didn't know him, and I don't need you to tell me what you felt he was or wasn't. I know what he was. How you saw him is irrelevant."

His lips parted and he stared at me in shock. I could imagine that he wanted nothing more than to turn, run from this house, and never look back. He was struggling to find words, but I didn't apologize and throw him a buoy.

"I didn't mean—"

"I know you didn't. I know you didn't, but just don't. Don't talk about him at all. What on earth made you think that you could have anything to say about him that would offer me solace? Why do you all keep trying to do that? What did you know about him?"

My voice was calm, but I could tell that every word cut the man like a dagger, and as I watched him retreat, I began to find myself again. It was time to ease off. I loosened my jaw and tried to visibly soften my expression. He stood staring at me. After several moments the blood began to return to his face, and he swallowed.

"I apologize," he said, doe-eyed and reaching behind him for the door handle. "I shouldn't have come. The last thing I meant to do was upset you."

I said nothing, expecting this was the period on the conversation, but he didn't make any further move to leave. I stared at him expectantly, waiting for him to go, but he didn't.

"It's fine," I offered, exhaling. "You caught me off guard, and to be truthful, I've been avoiding run-ins that would have resulted in a conversation exactly like this one. It isn't you—it's everything else. It's me, and it's him. You're right, you shouldn't have come here, but thank you."

He wasn't accustomed to this level of directness; I knew that about him. He was a sweet man, a farmer born and raised in this town, and a seemingly decent human being. The two of them had hit it off, though I was never sure why—they couldn't have been more different. I was merely a tagalong on the couple of occasions we had gotten together, but I had no problem with him and was happy to see them seemingly establish a connection. Even in my current state I knew this was a good man trying to do a good thing. I needed to pull myself through this, through a genuine interaction, before I got myself to a place where I'd never again be able to effectively communicate with another living human being. And if he'd truly liked this person, he would have wanted me to try right now.

I sighed. "You should dry off. You're cold." I gestured for him to come inside without looking him in the eye.

"No, no," he said, looking positively terrified. "No, I'm going to—"

"It's fine. Come in for a minute and I'll grab you a towel."

He didn't move. "Come in," I said, gesturing once more and showing my irritation. "I'd feel better about myself if you'd let me try to be kind to you, so just … come in."

He managed a small smile, which aggravated me more, but eventually he nodded, removed his shoes, and followed me sheepishly into the kitchen.

"Can I get you something?" I asked, with my back to him, making my way to the bathroom for a towel. "Water? Wine?"

I regretted the words the moment they left my mouth. It was a reflex that I'd assumed was dormant. The years of existing as a human who possessed social decency and manners had reared their ugly head, and without meaning to, I'd opened the door to something that made me feel sick to my stomach.

"Wine would be great, actually," he called after me.

I slammed down my hands on the washing machine, hidden from view behind the bathroom door. I closed my eyes and raised my face to the ceiling, cursing myself furiously under my breath. I stayed there with nothing but my self-hatred until I found the calm to once again attempt the role of a gracious human being. I emerged with a towel and handed it to him before walking to the living room. I retrieved one of the two remaining bottles of wine, which I'd been saving to bury myself in when needed, and returned to the kitchen with it and two glasses in hand. I'd need a sip of my own to get through this.

"So, I guess I shouldn't ... shouldn't ask how you are or nothin'."

I tried not to roll my eyes, but they moved without my consent. I considered apologizing but just poured wine into the glasses instead.

"I'm fine," I said. "I'm fine and I thank you for not asking."

He smiled again, though I hadn't intended to make him do so. He was charming and he was warm. In ordinary times I would have found him endearing. Now, however, I found him obnoxious. I would sooner have been in the company of someone with no tact nor compassion so that I'd not feel the need to try.

"And you?" I asked, taking an obviously large gulp of my wine. "You're well?"

He immediately seemed to relax, taking his own generous sip.

"Me? Yeah. Yeah, I'm good. Busy with the farm. Horses take up most of my time and I—"

"Did you talk much? Privately?" I asked sharply. "The two of you?"

The words left me before I had any intention of speaking at all. The wine, the utter stress of having to speak to another person face-to-face, and the sickening fact that I had allowed someone into our house—it had all cumulated in a minor eruption. I thought about retracting the question but for some reason felt compelled to leave it where it was.

"Oh," he said, once again looking afraid. "Yeah, I mean, we texted sometimes. Always trying to make plans, y'know, but we're all so busy. You guys have the shop and …"

He trailed off and just stared at me as I slowly nodded.

"Did you feel like you knew him, though?" I asked, almost sounding accusatory. "Was he a friend?"

To my surprise he didn't bumble through a response, but rather took another sip of wine and looked as though he was working hard to summon the right words.

"Did he seem happy to you?" I pressed, not knowing what I was doing or where I was taking this but dragging this man through it right along with me.

He took a deep breath and gave a nervous laugh. "I think he seemed tired?" he said, looking at me as though I was meant to agree. "He seemed tired?"

I nodded again, eyeing him as if he were prey. "And did he ever talk about us?"

He blew out an exaggerated breath. "Yeah? Yeah, sometimes," he said, running his finger around the rim of his glass. "But mostly just about the shop or what y'all were up to that weekend …"

I kept nodding, rapidly searching my brain for the next question. This was far too much, and he'd surely leave soon. I was scaring him and I was scaring myself, but a surge of aggression forced me to continue down this path. I was hungry for something.

"So you'd say he was happy," I said. "With me. In general, you'd say he was happy but tired?" I took another large sip.

He was folding; he knew he was not getting out without giving me something, anything. "Yeah, listen, I really didn't talk to him much, y'know? Never about anything important. I don't think I'd know if the guy was happy or not. I mean … I don't know. He seemed okay?"

The insanity that had momentarily consumed me began to subside, and I allowed myself to exhale. What was I doing to this person? I closed my eyes and slowly shook my head.

"I apologize," I said quietly. "I've lost myself these past few months. You're the first person I've spoken to in a long time who spent any time with him, and I suppose I was searching for something." I shook my head again. "Forgive me."

He looked bewildered, and as he took another sip of his wine, his wheels seemed to be turning. He sipped again. His cheeks were flushed.

"I wish I'd spent more time with you both," he said, with surprising confidence. "I liked you boys and wish we could have gotten to know each other better."

I softened under his sincerity. "That's very kind of you," I said, mustering a small smile. "I think he enjoyed talking to you too."

He nodded and looked down at his glass. His demeanour had changed, and I suddenly didn't recognize him. *This is a stranger*, I told myself. *This is essentially a stranger standing in our kitchen.*

When he looked up at me, his eyes had taken on a sort of mean-ness often seen in young men that would make them irresistible. He suddenly looked like a hunter, and I found myself regretting one more thing: I should not have offered him alcohol.

"But you didn't?" he asked. He took the final swig of his wine and roughly placed the glass on the counter.

I raised an eyebrow and waited for him to clarify what it was he'd just asked.

"Sorry," he said, laughing. "I'm sorry, man, that was … that was weird."

I narrowed my eyes. "I have no problem with you. I think I felt like the friendship was perhaps between the two of you and I was happy to join for a drink if and when."

He looked at me with a renewed sense of purpose. Something had shifted. I was unsure what was happening, but everything in the house suddenly seemed charged. The hairs on my neck stood on end.

He smiled a sly smile and I began to feel almost threatened. "Because I liked talking to you," he said, the wine exacerbating his drawl. "I liked you being there."

I raised an eyebrow again. "Okay," I said flatly. "That's nice of you."

He nervously scratched at his neck and then made a fist with his hand. "I mean, I really liked you being there, a lot." His gaze locked on mine. "I mean, I never would have meant any disrespect, and I know you two had been together a long while, but … gosh, I don't have much experience with this, sorry." He laughed again, looking at me for some sort of validation.

He playfully tapped his knuckles on the counter as though signalling he was ready to move this conversation to the next stage of whatever the hell this was. I felt dizzy; I felt danger. Without my love here, without my protector, I was wide open and alone. A sense of static began to fill the room, and a tingle ran up my spine. Every inanimate object felt alive instantly and I found myself clenching my fists. He took the wine bottle and refilled his glass, then took another large sip as I watched without saying a word.

"You're a handsome man, y'know?" he said, leering at me, his hand now working its way across the counter toward my fist.

"And, again, I wouldn't want to overstep or nothin', but maybe sometime down the road, y'know, when you're feeling better—"

The wineglass exploded in his hand. Shards scattered. The remaining wine splattered up his arm and across the front of his shirt, leaving him looking as though he'd just been impaled. He yelped in pain and grasped the hand that had been holding the glass as he recoiled from the counter. Blood streamed from his palm, and he winced as the severity of the cut became apparent.

"Fuck!" he yelled. "What the—"

He was cut off by the whooshing sound of all four burners on the stove lighting at full strength. He spun around to look and then whipped back around to face me, waiting for an explanation. I simply stared, my gaze moving from the flames to his bleeding hand.

"What ..." he said, still clutching his hand, his chest heaving.

I came to and rushed past him to turn off the burners, but again the knobs were in the off position and there was nothing I could do.

"You need to leave," I said.

He gaped. "Are you gonna fuckin' help me at least?" he asked, flabbergasted.

I glanced at the counter, picked up the towel he'd used to dry himself, and then tossed it at him.

"Wrap it in this until you get home," I said. "You have to go now."

He stared at me for a few seconds before shaking his head in disbelief. I was emboldened. I felt like an army was at my back, and I felt a rage that wasn't my own. Wrapping his wound, he headed for the entrance. He turned to me before the door closed behind him, about to speak. I cut him off.

"It's not just your timing," I said coldly. "He told me about guys like you, boys that terrified him and then took advantage of his weakness when no one was looking. We've all known guys like you. You fucking straight hillbillies who've never had the backbone to seek out a life for yourself and think that after a shot of whisky, the local faggot is fair game. Like he's here for your sexual target practice and when you're done, you can go back to tormenting him."

His eyes widened as I continued. "If he were here, he'd have knocked your fucking teeth out, you disrespectful, closet-case dope. You're goddamn lucky I didn't do it myself. Don't ever speak his name again and don't you ever come back here. Ever."

The door closed, and I watched his silhouette move from the front steps to the driveway. His tires squealed. Thunder rolled. Rain pounded the living room window. Briefly, I wondered if I'd dreamt the last fifteen minutes. I waited for my body and mind to fall back into step with each other. Then I looked toward the kitchen, a smile slowly spreading across my face.

"Babe," I whispered, in a mildly scolding tone, unable to conceal a small laugh.

Venturing into the kitchen to clean up another shattered glass, I felt alive, filled with the exhilaration I'd always felt when his love was at its most untamed.

2022

"I'M FINE," I said, taking him by his shoulders. "It's only a precaution. I'm fine and you know that."

He shook himself free of me, agitated and overcome with worry. "I don't know that and neither do you. Your head could be hanging half off your fucking neck, and you'd say the same thing."

I tried not to smile. He had a tendency to take the things he found worth worrying about—which was most things—and blow them far out of proportion. He was afraid, though, so I endeavoured to tread carefully.

"There's no reason to believe there's anything wrong with me," I said. "I'll see my doctor and come home to you the same day, fully intact."

"When's the last time someone you knew found a lump on their body and everything was just tickety-fucking-boo?" he asked angrily. "Cancer runs like wildfire through your fucking family."

I closed my eyes, feeling both the hit of truth in that statement as well as the early onset of exhaustion. I knew how much energy it would take to walk through this with him. I whispered his name, opened my eyes, and placed my hands on his shoulders.

"Right now, there's nothing to worry about. I feel great—better than ever. It's just that I'd be remiss if I didn't get an opinion. The appointment is in two weeks, and—"

"Two weeks! Two fucking weeks we're supposed to wait? No. No, that's unacceptable."

"Baby, this is the state of things. You know that," I said, in a soothing tone. "Even if it is something, which it isn't, two weeks isn't going to make a difference—"

"The fuck it isn't," he snapped. "Give me your doctor's phone number right now." He held out his hand.

"Stop it," I said calmly. "It's a small lump on my rib. There are many possibilities other than the one you're so eager to jump to."

This took him aback, as I'd intended it to. He could become so swallowed up in his emotional responses that he'd end up being blatantly insensitive toward the very person he was trying to help. It would be the last thing he ever intended to do, but at times his worry knew no boundaries.

He exhaled and relaxed his shoulders. "I'm sorry. I'm sorry, I shouldn't be filling your head with this. But you can't be as dismissive of this as you are of everything else that scares you. This can't wait two weeks, and I'd really like you to call back and push for something sooner. Please?"

I let myself smile this time, taking him all in. I was lucky to have him. He would care for me until it killed him.

"How many times have I watched you bust an ankle, a foot, a knee while running and then proceed to ignore my every request to go and have it checked out?" I asked.

"If I stop running, I'll get fat and you'll leave me and no one else will want me, so I've no choice but to push through." He rolled his eyes. "Always, always remain in the game, no matter how bad it hurts," he said, with mock sincerity that I knew was, in fact, mostly genuine.

I laughed and pulled him roughly toward me, wrapping my arms around him and then burying my face in his neck. He immediately returned the embrace and placed a hand comfortingly on the back of my head. We stayed this way for nearly a minute before he spoke.

"Whatever it is or isn't, I've got you," he said, his voice cracking slightly. "You know that, yes?"

I nodded, my face still nestled between his neck and shoulder.

"I've got you and you don't need to worry."

"I'm not worried," I reminded him. "You're the one already planning my funeral."

"I have my dress picked out and everything. Full-scale wailing before I throw myself onto the casket."

"I want to be cremated. You know that."

He shrugged. "Lots of local taxidermists. I have other plans."

Two weeks later, I returned late at night from my appointment in the city. I crept in, hoping not to wake him—a needless gesture, as I knew there was no chance he'd slept. In fact, I was surprised to find him in bed at all. It was raining, and he'd opened the bedroom windows. A breeze gently blew the curtains. It was more comfort than I'd felt all day, and I was so grateful for him and the house in that moment that I found myself almost choking up.

"Hi," I whispered, as I crawled on top of him. I allowed my full weight to settle on his body.

He grunted, then put his arms around me. We'd spoken and texted throughout the day. I was fine, there was nothing more to report, and I was glad to be able to just lie with him now. His eyes were cloudy, and I knew it was possible he'd taken something for his nerves. I never encouraged it, but right now I was thankful. His ease would help me to settle into mine.

"You okay?" he asked groggily.

I nodded into his chest, rubbing my scruff against his pecs before placing the right side of my face against them.

"What can I do?"

"Nothing," I said with a sigh. "Sleep. You can sleep."

He was struggling to breathe but did not try to move from under me.

"Did they mention anything about your weight?" he asked quietly.

I laughed for the first time in days and felt so overwhelmed with love for him that once again I nearly began to cry.

"Yes. They told me to keep at it."

"Fuck's sake. I'll die like this."

I laughed again and rolled off him onto my side. He turned to face me and rubbed his hand along my bicep, gradually transitioning to gliding just a finger up and down the length of my arm.

"Are you really okay?" he asked, his eyes on mine.

"I am," I said, and touched his face before extending my neck to kiss him. "I'm with you."

He found my hand and clasped it tightly, bringing it to his chest.

"I love you so much," he said, his eyes glistening.

"I love you too," I said, pulling myself as close to his body as I could.

I could see that he was trying to find words. He was worrying, and he was thinking, and he was likely as exhausted as I was. No doubt he'd tortured himself all day with thoughts of what might lie ahead for us. When he spoke, it was from a place that caused me to be still. The sentiment wasn't unfamiliar, but I'd never heard the words spoken with such conviction.

"I have to go first. I don't want to know what life is without you. I have to go first."

I brushed his hair away and softly kissed his forehead. "No one is going anywhere."

"I mean it," he replied, the weight of his thoughts and the pill he might have taken seemingly allowing him to speak with complete calm. "Don't leave me here. I can't do this without you."

"What can't you do without me?" I asked. A gentle challenge. He was capable of far more than he'd ever realized.

"Us," he replied. "I can't be you and me without you, and you and me is everything. I have to go first because living without you would kill me anyway."

I fell asleep a short time later and awoke only once to the sensation of his finger slowly tracing my spine.

May 2024

THE SCENT OF the neighbouring farmlands had settled over the town, as it did each spring. The yard remained dull, but there were buds in the trees. I had relaxed into a new way of life throughout the final days of April. He had made it clear that he still considered this house, and me, his territory, so I had accepted that he and I would remain in our home together the way we now were. This would be enough for me. I had debated selling the house, and had spent many hours trying to envision what my life without him could look like if I were to find the strength to leave. It didn't look good. There was no place I could go where I wouldn't wish he were there with me, or I were here with him.

I made a plan for the gardens and some minor home repairs we'd put off, and I intended to spend May setting about these tasks. I even considered the idea of venturing into the city to gather supplies to make the enhancements to the bedroom we'd spoken about many times. If he was going to stay here with me, maybe I could continue to care for our home the way we'd set out to. I wanted him to be happy here. These projects would also help establish a sense of normalcy that would permit me to stay with him while retaining purpose. My hope was that this would prevent me from spending my days wine soaked and tucked away in the basement, waiting for him to come to me. I was surviving off of our remaining income from the sale of the condo back in the city, but remained cautious while considering these investments. Something his incessant worry had taught me: never to feel entirely secure.

It had been two weeks since he drove our presumed friend out of the house, and I hadn't seen any evidence of him since. I spoke to him often. Sometimes I'd even ask him a question as though there were the possibility that he'd respond. That I'd hear his voice behind me offering a sharp-tongued reply. That I'd laugh and turn to find him there. I spoke to him of my plans for the gardens and wondered if he could show signs of disagreement or if something so petty wasn't a part of this deal.

I stood outside the back door, sipping my coffee out of sight of the neighbours. I took in the spring breeze and imagined the gardens weeks from now. Doing so didn't sicken me, as it would have weeks earlier. I was feeling as though in some way, we'd be spending our summer here together. Just as I began falling into a daydream, I was hit with a wave of fatigue that drained me of all ambition. I'd been sleeping better but could still lie awake for hours, thinking about him. I knew that this, more than anything, had taken a dire toll on my mental health, and for the first time I was able to empathize with how he must have felt spending all those years deprived of proper sleep. I cursed myself for the nights I knew had been the result of my wrong-doing. I wished over and over that I could go back and find him on those evenings. He'd needed me then, and I was ashamed for the times I'd turned my back on him.

I stepped back inside and slid the screen door closed behind me. He'd always wanted as much fresh air as possible to flow through the house and would leave the windows open until he could no longer stand the chill. Then he'd curse the cool nights and move from room to room, closing the windows. I put down my mug on the kitchen table, rubbed my eyes, and made my way upstairs, deciding I'd lie in our bed until I felt recharged enough to work on my to-do list.

The sounds, smells, and breeze I'd enjoyed outside welcomed me into our bedroom, and the curtains gently played about. I smiled as I lay on the bed, imagining him standing there looking out at his yard. He'd eventually choose me over the view. He'd cross the room to climb on top of my body, then he'd nestle in, kiss my neck, and create a nook for himself inside my arm. He'd lay his head on my chest and either begin to talk at me or remain lost in his daydreams.

"I love you," I whispered, as I drifted off.

It was dark when I woke, and the room had cooled. Disoriented, I rolled over and reached for my phone on his nightstand. It was 8:20 p.m., too late to bother trying to eat a meal but too early to attempt to sleep through the night. I lay still for several minutes, the churning sensation that took hold of my stomach every evening beginning to surface. During the day, I could keep busy. Late at night, I could wonder if he'd return to me again. But these hours in between were a void. This was when I felt the despair as fresh and relentless as it had been in the days immediately following his death.

I ran through possible ways to pass the time, and they all involved wine. I glanced at the window. The cool air had lost its promise of spring. I would get up, I would close the window, and I would go downstairs. I would start there.

Several minutes passed. I pulled his pillow to me and wrapped my arms around it. I thought back to the first night he visited me, his silhouette illuminated by a winter moon and his naked body facing the night as though that darkness was now his home. I saw his beautiful face as it turned toward me and felt a pang of guilt and remorse, recalling how I'd recoiled in fear. I hoped he wasn't wounded by my reaction then.

"I'm sorry," I whispered, still gazing toward the window.

As I recounted the events of the last four months, I was reminded of the shattered photo. I'd tucked it away in the drawer of his nightstand, vowing to replace the frame. As I hadn't left the house for more than a few late-night supply runs when the generosity of others ran out, this hadn't happened. I propped myself up, reached over, and slowly opened the drawer. I found the photo where I'd left it, resting on top of a collection of greeting cards he'd saved along with a few other items I hadn't explored, still determined to respect his privacy.

There we were, locked in a kiss, the city and the possibilities of our future together lighting the sky behind us. His smile was so sincere, and I was fairly certain he'd laughed after the kiss. We were filled with the joy of the holidays, the charge of the city, and our love for one another. We were beautiful, and I was again reminded that even at our worst, we still found happiness together.

I stared at the photo for a spell and then decided it would do no harm to see what else he'd stored in this drawer. I wanted to see which of the many cards I'd written him he'd decided to keep. I knew that each would fill me with a gut-wrenching memory, and that's what I wanted. If he wouldn't come to me tonight, I'd bring myself as close to him—as close to us—as I could.

I brushed aside several cards and took a quick look at a couple of photos. They were of us, but they had no apparent significance. I then pulled one card from the small pile and opened it, resting my head on the pillow. I'd given it to him on his birthday close to ten years ago, and in it I'd written that I couldn't wait to see what the year ahead had in store for him. He never believed me, but I truly believed in him. Every failure he thought he'd suffered, I'd seen as a brave attempt at living a full life with as few regrets as possible. He chose trying over hiding, no matter the hit he took for it, and I'd always believed that one day it would pay off for him. I'd still have believed that now.

I ran my finger over the card, caressing the words *I love you* absentmindedly. After placing it beside me on the bed, I lazily reached over to retrieve another from the drawer. As I fumbled, my fingers came across something that wasn't a card or a photo. The shape felt familiar. I clasped it and lifted it from the drawer. As my brain registered the object in my hand, my heart sank and my stomach turned.

An ache clamped down on my chest, and a lump formed in my throat. It was a ring box, black velvet, with a small piece of paper protruding from one side. It was out of place here, and for a moment I tried to make myself believe it had been left in the drawer accidentally by someone else. Even at my most delusional and desperate, though, I'd never let myself go to that extent. This was his.

I stared at the box, heartsick and knowing that everything I'd thought I'd known was once again about to be taken from me. My newfound peace broke apart, as did my commitment to live out my days coexisting with him in our home this way. Tears welled in my eyes, and I forced myself to open the box.

The piece of paper fell to the bed, leaving behind a white-gold ring with four diamonds running diagonally across the band. It was simple, it was modest, and it was one of the most beautiful things I'd ever seen. He had chosen this ring for me. He'd likely had no idea what he was looking for, but he'd seen this, and he'd chosen it for me.

I lost my breath and for a moment thought I might be sick. I couldn't bring myself to touch it. I gently set the box on the mattress in front of my chest while I attempted to catch my breath, the ring staring up at me. I glanced at the scrap of paper and willed myself to take it in my hand. The paper had been folded several times, and I fumbled trying to open it with trembling hands and blurred vision.

On it were three lines with strikes through several words and replacements written above them. I moaned as I realized that this was his proposal to me. He'd written and revised it on this crumpled piece of paper and tucked it away with the ring for safekeeping. I had no idea how long the ring had been here or when he'd planned to propose. It was something we'd only recently talked about. For most of our relationship, we'd shared the view that marriage was unnecessary. After thirteen years, we were only just seeming to open ourselves to the idea that we were truly forever in every possible sense and that maybe it was finally time to prove that to one another.

My body shook as I read his words over and over. I could hear his voice in them, could envision what his face, his mouth, his eyes would have looked like as he spoke them. He'd have been filled with anxiety and possibly the fear of rejection; he may have cried while trying to recite the words. Despite everything we were and had been through, he'd still have wondered if I was truly his and if he was capable of making me happy.

I collapsed from the inside out. I grabbed the ring box and clutched it so tightly that I thought it would break. Holding it against my chest, I began to sob uncontrollably. I shook my head, wanting to refuse this discovery and wishing that I could have back the pain I'd felt ten minutes prior rather than the agony that ravaged me now.

I hadn't known him. I hadn't known this was possible. I hadn't known he'd truly wanted this, and what was worse was that I'd been so close to having it. I had been a measurable time from committing every part of myself to him for the rest of my life, and I had wanted that. But I'd never spoken it, and he'd died not knowing this.

I summoned all the pain I was feeling and screamed into the darkness of our bedroom, my cry carrying out of his open window and into the night. I buried my tear-stained face in his pillow and screamed again and again, punching the mattress furiously. I wouldn't survive this. We would never be engaged, and we would never marry. We weren't going to live out our days together in our home, and I'd never know what the future had held for us, because it was gone.

Hours passed. Dawn crept into the room, shedding just enough light for me to know that the day was nearly upon me. At some point in the night I'd stopped crying, stopped screaming, and had gone numb. I hadn't let go of the ring box for even a second and had spent much of the time envisioning what marriage might have meant for us. But at some point I'd come to a familiar realization: He was never coming home to me. Our time together here had ended, and though I could remain here with him as we were now, I'd never be happy. He'd also never be happy this way, having a part of me but never being able to grab hold of every ounce of me.

It was then, through the first glow of early morning light, that he came to me. He stood in front of his window, again wearing nothing and staring out into the beyond. He didn't turn to look at me, and I didn't speak. I could see tears streaming down his right cheek, and they began to flow from my own eyes once again. We stayed this way for what felt like an eternity before he turned his head toward me, a look of purest heartache upon his face. My eyes pled *I'm sorry*, but I said nothing. He turned slowly back toward the window, and then he was gone.

2023

I WATCHED HIM sip his cocktail and stare toward the long grass lining our wooden fence. I could almost see the summer breeze slowing his busy mind to a crawl. He gently placed his glass on the ground beside his chair and leaned his head back, closing his eyes.

We'd find ourselves in this hidden corner of our backyard every Sunday by late afternoon, when we both felt ready to allow the work and worries of the week to finally set us down. It was our sanctuary, and it was one of the few times and spaces where he seemed content to just be—he'd speak to me very little. A small table separated the chair and the love seat that we each occupied: He preferred to curl into the chair and appreciate the view of our yard offered by its position; I preferred the love seat, and the view it offered me of him.

I put down the book we'd been sharing and continued to observe him. He opened his eyes just a little, sensing mine on him, and smiled.

"Creep," he grumbled. The sun had added weight to his voice.

I stretched my leg toward him and nudged his with my foot, smiling.

"What do you want?" he said with a laugh.

I ran my toe up and down his shin. "You're better here."

He turned his head to face me and cocked it slightly. "We're better here."

He returned his gaze to the tall grass and took a deep breath. He was right. We had settled into one another and into us as a unit in a way we never had in years past. There would always be disagreements. We would forever remain in love but often at odds. But in our third summer here in this yard, surrounded by the sounds of birds, the colours of our gardens, and the vines of his pumpkins, which had nearly engulfed the chair he now sat upon, we felt at peace.

It frightened me to admit it, but I was beginning to feel tired. Time and wear and tear on my body were leaving me to wonder how much fight I'd have left in me if he and I were to ever find ourselves at a bridge as difficult as those we'd had to cross so many times before. I didn't want that for us anymore. My need to establish space and remain my own island had dissolved into the need to take care of him and us. More so than ever before, keeping him happy was my primary purpose.

"You're right, though," he said, breaking my chain of thought. "I've been better lately. Much better."

I smiled a small smile and felt a sense of relief knowing that he too believed he was more at ease as of late. The storm that raged inside of him would often reveal itself during periods of seeming serenity, so I could never be certain as to how he was doing. His words gave me hope that perhaps he was turning a corner.

"I haven't had a panic attack in a few months," he said, "and I haven't needed a sedative since Christmas. I don't know why. Nothing's changed. I just feel ... better." He rewarded himself with a smile.

I nodded. "I wish you could sleep more." This continued to be a problem that plagued him and was the culprit behind his sometimes-short temper and his tendency to drift into worry where there was no need for any. He seemed better, but the demons would always remain, and they found their opening in those hours he lay awake.

"I'm sorry," he said, his smile fading. "I keep you awake."

"No. No, you don't. I just feel you when you are."

He turned away but wrapped his foot behind my ankle, letting me know he was still here with me. He settled his gaze on the garden to his left.

"Thank you," he said quietly.

"What for?"

He waited several seconds before answering. "Our life. You promised me that one day it would be better and that it would all be worth it." He turned to face me again. "And it is."

A part of me couldn't trust what he was saying. I had wanted this all along, to see him this way and for both of us to feel this level of contentment, but after the years of uncertainty, broken trust, and his feelings of hopelessness, that he could now believe we'd live a happy life together seemed impossible.

"I know you have regrets," I said. "I wish we'd made different decisions and made them sooner. I'm sorry for the time I cost you."

"Babe," he said, in a mildly scolding tone but giving me a reassuring look. "We wasted a lot of time, but we're here now. We could have done any one thing differently, but then we might not have ended up here, together, just like this. And this, right now, is what I want."

My heart was heavy, but so full. "Do you truly mean that?"

He lifted himself from his chair and moved to the love seat to straddle me. He kissed me gently, then looked into my eyes and smiled.

"It's you and me," he said. "Yeah?"

I buried my face in his chest and wrapped him tightly in my arms. "You and me."

That evening we spread out a blanket in the grass and lay on our backs, our eyes to the skies.

A meteor shower was set to peak that night, and he'd talked about us stargazing for days now. It was a clear, humid night, and the breeze we'd enjoyed that afternoon had died down, leaving just us and the sound of the crickets. The blanket was large but despite the heat, we pressed the sides of our bodies together. He was quiet. He had been for the remainder of the day. Any time this happened, I knew he had much to say but was either trying to find the right words or believing that he was sparing me the chatter—I could have listened to him empty his thoughts all night long, though. Always.

"I miss the city sometimes," he said dreamily. "But I think I'd miss this more."

I smiled. Any reassurance that he felt as at home here as I did, filled me with joy.

"There's more room for imagination here," he continued. "I feel like I can daydream again. Do you know what I mean?" He turned his head to face me, waiting for me to respond.

I said nothing, and enjoyed the very idea of him lost in a fantasy somewhere inside of himself.

He grunted in displeasure with my silence. "Why do you make it so hard, talking to you about these things?" he asked, caressing my arm with his finger.

"What things?" I asked, my gaze fixed on the stars.

"I don't know. All of the things that exist in the spaces between everything we're supposed to know and do. It's hard to want to talk about things that I know you have no room for. It makes me sad that you refuse to let your mind play every now and then."

"Sweetheart," I said with a sigh. "What do you want to talk about?"

He was pensive a moment, and seemed embarrassed. "Meteors," he said quietly. "Shooting stars, space, life here and life elsewhere. Just everything that's possibly out there. I wish we could see it—all of it."

"I never said that I had no room for that. I told you I believe in the possibility of things, but without seeing proof of them myself ..."

"You've seen proof. You just choose not to believe."

"Are the Martians coming?" I asked mockingly.

He chuckled. "Maybe. They could. You can't honestly believe it's just us here though, do you?"

I sighed, disappointed that in my wine-induced haze I was going to have to give him the focus he'd need to see this conversation through.

"I believe in the possibility," I repeated.

"But it's pretty arrogant to believe that there's no way anything but us could exist out there. You have to agree that there's no reason we should be the only ones able to sustain life on a planet."

As he aged, he got better at cornering me with rational thought versus hyper emotion. He knew I couldn't disagree with this statement but also knew he was challenging me and leaving me no choice but to respond.

"Can we just look at the stars?" I asked.

"No," he said, rolling his body toward me and resting his head on my chest. "I want you to talk to me about these things. Why do you refuse to believe in anything?"

Another shot to the heart, but twelve years in I took these less personally, knowing that he never intended to be hurtful. He genuinely wanted me to explain myself.

"Don't you want to believe in anything?" he pressed. "Don't you want to just let yourself believe that there's more than just this and us?"

I stroked his hair with the hand belonging to the arm pinned beneath him.

"I like this and us," I said, craning my neck to kiss the top of his head.

"Stop. I mean it. Do you really not believe in anything more than what you can see? You really, honestly, don't think there's anything more out there? Or right here?"

The conversation we'd had while driving out of Savannah flashed through my mind, and I felt tension run up my spine. The impacts of our disagreements had taken root in our bodies and would sometimes remind us of their existence.

"Baby," I said softly. "Don't get upset. You can just lie here and watch shooting stars with me and that can be enough. You don't need to think, and you don't need to worry and wonder—you can just be here with me and that can be enough. You can just enjoy this and it's okay."

He fell quiet, and his breathing softened. He adjusted himself so that he could see the stars. We lay there for several minutes, and then, finally, a meteor blazed across the night sky almost directly in line with the top of our house. He put his hand on my chest and gripped it with exhilaration. I could feel his state of being lighten. He was almost childlike. I turned my head to see him smiling at the sky, his eyes twinkling. He relaxed again and let out a long breath.

"There's more," he whispered. "I don't care if you believe it or not." He looked at me and ruffled my hair gently. "There's more and one day you'll see it."

May 2024

I BEGAN BY sorting through our closets and filling garbage bags with items neither of us had worn in recent memory. This part hurt as much as I had expected it to. He was in the air that filled my lungs, not the sweater I now shoved into a bag. I knew this, but I would catch the scent of him on a sweater and find myself paralyzed for several moments before forcing myself to come to and carry on. Anything that didn't end up in these bags for charity, I'd leave hanging or folded. These items would be part of a much larger decision that I'd make when I was ready to do so.

Next, I boxed his CD and movie collection, leaving out the handful of films we'd watched on rotation with one another. Any music that reminded me of him I could find on demand, so I rationalized that the disc library itself held no value to me. Whenever I felt a pang of guilt, I reminded myself that these weren't the things that had made him what he was to me. Removing them from the house didn't remove him from me.

I set about these tasks determined but finding no relief. These were simply things that needed to be done so we could move forward. We weren't okay this way. The belief I'd had while under the influence of grief and desperation—that we could continue on as we were—was harmful to us both. I didn't know where this was heading or where I'd stop but for now, I needed to take these steps without pausing to question my expectations.

I spent several days identifying things that held no sentimental value to me, and packing them away. Slowly, the house began to look as though we were either moving out or moving in, and try as I might, I couldn't prevent myself from reliving the day of our move-in. We'd had only a few belongings with us. The movers would arrive the following morning. We spent that first night on an air mattress in our new bedroom, locked together through the sleepless hours, feeling as though there was nothing and no one left in the world but us, and I'd loved it. At one point I crept downstairs, believing he'd finally fallen asleep. I'd wanted some time to survey the house and take it in but true to form, he'd come down and retrieved me and then took me back to our empty room filled with nothing but each other. That night, his need for us to stay close had reassured me that we could do this together—that we were the team I'd always believed us to be.

I sat down on the couch and stared at the three boxes I'd placed against the wall in the living room. Once more I told myself that this was good, this was causing him no harm, and if anything, he'd appreciate that I was taking care of things. He'd never liked loose ends, and though he'd struggled with endings themselves, he'd always ensured that they were quick and final. He knew that a good time could never be preserved and believed that trying to do so rendered it stale and overstayed.

I considered a glass of wine but knew that it was too early in the day and wouldn't help anything. Numbing the anxiety of not knowing what to do now would only keep it waiting for me the morning after. This was when he would have stepped in and told us what to do. He would have instructed me and pushed us to get the job finished for fear of it remaining undone and causing him to lie awake thinking about it. Once again, as I did all day every day, I needed him.

Confining myself to the house was limiting the number of things I could see and do that would make me feel close to him again. I had devoured every memory here, and I felt a little less impacted each time I tried to summon him back into my body and mind via a glance out the window or an inhale of his face cream. I wanted to stay in this place where he filled every room, but I also had to learn to move forward while still keeping him close.

I conversed with myself for a few minutes before concluding that I'd go for a walk. I'd retrace the steps we'd taken together so many evenings. I'd walk the paths we'd enjoyed in the summer sun. Sometimes we hid beer in his backpack to drink in the woods, as though we were high school kids. This was how I'd feel him again in ways I'd since forgotten. Feeling almost as though he were next to me and in agreement that we should take this stroll, I pulled myself from the couch, found my sneakers, and set out into the mild May air.

It was a beautiful evening, so I knew that many of the locals would be making use of the trails. To avoid contact, as we'd always done, I skulked around corners and kept my eyes peeled for landmines in the form of anyone who'd stop me to talk, feeling certain they'd know just what to say. This led me on an indirect route to a portion of the trails that would be mostly, if not entirely, free of fellow travellers. I didn't mind the reroutes. I saw reminders of him down every quiet street and pathway. Already it was working.

I heard him whispering a venomous remark about a neighbour we'd agreed to dislike, and smiled at the thought of how much he'd made me laugh when he shouldn't have been encouraged. I saw him walking ahead of me, lost in a daydream, as we crossed the soccer field. I felt him next to me every step, and this gave me a renewed sense of faith that even though I knew we couldn't go on this way, he was and would remain close.

I passed through the empty college grounds and eventually arrived at the opening of the wooded trail I'd vowed not to return to. The image of his blood-soaked body that morning he'd come to me had shaken me each and every day since. Whatever the reason he'd stopped me from getting closer to the place where he'd died, his reaction had been sufficient for me not to try. He'd asked me to stop, so I had. And I'd promised us both I wouldn't return.

Now here I stood, the familiar tree-lined tunnel looming ahead and the spot where he'd left me just around a slight bend, out of sight. What beauty I'd once found in this trail had been replaced by darkness and violence. I was staring into the monster that had stolen my love, when my phone rang. The sound startled me slightly, as it rang far less these days. Those closest to me had begun to drift. I pulled the phone from my back pocket and glanced at the call display to see the name of his best friend.

I'd spoken to him infrequently despite his being the only other person I could imagine might be experiencing anything similar to the level of loss I was suffering. Their friendship had been a unique one, and although we'd all spent a great deal of time together, I had remained on the periphery. That had been fine with me, but the unfortunate side effect was that I was never entirely sure how to speak to this person.

As I stood paralyzed at the base of the trail, undecided as to whether I'd return home or continue down a new path, I wondered if speaking to him would help push me in one direction or the other. We weren't unsimilar when it came to our emotional hurdles, and if there was anyone with whom I could stomach the conversations I needed to have, it was him. My love had been drawn both to emotionally unavailable lovers and emotionally unavailable friends.

I answered the call and said hi.

"Oh great, you picked up," he said sarcastically. "Now I'm gonna have to think of shit to say."

I chuckled and was suddenly relieved to be hearing from him. I had forgotten what it was like to want a conversation to unfold.

"I should have called you again sooner," I said. "I apologize. I mean, I'm not actually that sorry, but I apologize."

He mustered his own laugh and sighed. "So? How are you doing?"

"I'm fine," I lied. "Trying to keep busy and … I'm fine."

"Sure. You've been holed away in that house for the better part of four months, not answering or returning phone calls, and you've probably gotten pretty fat and likely smell atrocious."

"I'm not fat, and I stopped noticing the smell weeks ago."

He laughed again, but it was broken. He was trying. It was his nature to allow sarcasm to carry an entire dialogue, though, so I knew I needed to find the strength within myself to truly talk to him—no matter how uncomfortable it made us both.

"Are you okay?" I asked. "You holding up?"

He was silent for a few moments, and when he replied, his tone was muffled and filled with resignation. "No, I'm not really that okay but neither are you and neither of us is going to talk about it, so for the sake of us both getting through this call, I'll just say yeah, I'm good."

"I have a few of his things for you if you want them," I said. "I can drive them down next time I come to the city."

I'd been too direct, and it had silenced him. The poor man wouldn't know the appropriate question to ask next. This had become a trend with me now, silencing well-meaning people with a direct hit.

"There's nothing of note," I continued. "You both grew up in the same era of music, so I thought you might want some of his CDs. There are a couple of necklaces I thought might remind you of him as well. I'd be happy for you to have them."

"Are you moving?" he finally asked.

"No. I don't know. I need to do something, but I don't know if I have it in me to leave the house."

"Understandable. You guys created a life there for yourselves, and it would be really hard to leave it behind. I was jealous of you both. Surprised it worked out, but jealous."

I clucked my displeasure. "Come on."

"No, I am—was really happy for you guys. The years of hearing him vent about what an asshole you were, I wasn't sure how this venture would pan out, but you both seemed really happy. I mean, as happy as he could seem, given this is him we're talking about. But it was nice to see him like that. He seemed calmer the last couple of years. He grew up a lot."

"He was. Calmer. He found himself here, I think."

There was an awkward silence as we both struggled to determine where to go next. I was still staring down the trail, kicking my feet in the gravel like a nervous child. The vision of him lying wounded in the snow hit me fast and hard, and words spoke themselves before I could attempt to shape them.

"I don't know what to do here," I said, my voice cracking, which likely shocked his friend as much as it shocked me. "I don't know what I'm supposed to do, and I feel this immense pressure to move in one direction or another and I don't know where to go from here."

He was quiet for a long while, and that was fair. He'd need time to consider how to respond to this outpouring. This conversation wasn't one that either of us was equipped for, yet I was thrusting us into it and asking him to keep up.

"I have days where I feel like I can still salvage a life here," I continued. "But I can't, and I feel like I'm failing him—us—by not keeping everything as he'd built it. The house, the shop, our routines … I don't know what I can do to keep him alive anymore because it's killing me trying to."

After a few more seconds of silence he cleared his throat, letting me know he was, in fact, still on the line. "I think," he began slowly, "that he would want you to be happy—"

"Oh for fuck's sake," I said, instantly exasperated. "Everyone says that, don't they? *He'd just want you to be happy.* Or, *he'd just be happy knowing that you're happy.* I didn't answer your call so that I could do this again. Not with you."

"Okay—"

"Maybe he doesn't want me to be happy. You know? Maybe he doesn't want that at all. Maybe he's angry or he's scared and maybe every time I try to move forward it hurts him. Maybe I'm just hurting him. Maybe I'm hurting him all the time and all he wants is to be with me, here, as we were."

"Okay. Maybe."

I paused and then realized I'd hoped for more in response. Embarrassment washed over me. I'd cornered him. I collected myself in the silence that followed and took some deep breaths, looking toward the path.

"I apologize," I said. "I haven't spoken to anyone about this. Any of it. Clearly I should have."

"It's fine," he replied, in an even tone. "Don't apologize, but I can't make sense of your grief for you. I can't make sense of mine. There's a hole here and I don't know how to fix it, so I'm sorry if I don't know what to say. Blind leading the blind, you know?"

"I know. I didn't mean to put this on you. I know this has been difficult for you as well."

"The city still reminds me of him," he said. "The shitty places he'd make me eat and drink, the park we'd all party in every Pride. I wasn't nostalgic for any of it when you guys left, but for some reason, knowing he's never coming back made it hurt to be here. I feel him more now than I ever did in the four years since you left."

I was relieved by his honesty. He'd met me where I was, and this offering put me at ease.

This was what it meant to lose love: It left a mark on everything, everywhere, all the time.

I knew that he'd want to hang up soon and felt suddenly panicked. I wanted to tell him everything that had been happening. I wanted a person with strength who'd known us both to hear it. I couldn't, though. I couldn't get myself to that point, as there was no returning from it.

"Thank you," I said instead. "For telling me that. And I apologize again for making you uncomfortable."

"Yeah, no, I'm never calling this number again," he said. I laughed through my own discomfort. "And don't call here either."

"I won't, I promise," I replied, smiling.

"Honestly though?" he said, surprising me. I'd thought he'd be eager to abandon the conversation now. "It sounds as though nothing has changed."

My smile faded. The impending sunset began to settle itself into the woods ahead of me.

"You can't live with him and you can't move on without him," he continued. "You were both the same. There was this constant tug-of-war between the two of you. Anyone on the outside could have seen it was time to maybe give up, but you two just couldn't stay away from each other. I gave up figuring it out early on and just assumed you'd sort out your shit, come what may. Maybe you still haven't, though."

Though the words themselves weren't poetic, their impact silenced me. It was the first outside perspective I'd allowed room for since he died.

"Anyway," he said, clearing the air between us. "I am here if you need to call and be weird again. You know that, yeah?"

"Yeah," I said, feeling a chill run through me as the air cooled and the trail continued to darken. "You too. I'll even answer. Maybe."

We said our goodbyes, and as I returned the phone to my pocket, I felt no desire to walk toward the dimming trail. Instead, I turned and made my way back to our home, my head hung low and my hands in my pockets. The streets were quiet. I was glad not to have encountered anyone.

I felt I'd been scolded but also awakened. I was in fact doing to him what I always had, and he was obliging. Neither of us felt we could survive without the other, no matter how great the fight. For four months I'd called to him, and he'd answered. Was it all my fault? Or had he never really left me?

I pushed open the front door and stepped inside, feeling as though I were coming home to him. The feeling was so concrete that he could have been standing in the kitchen, waiting for me, and I wouldn't have startled. I moved slowly from room to room, hoping if not expecting to see him. Finally, I stopped and stood in the centre of the living room—the exact place where he'd wrapped himself around me on Valentine's Day.

I stared out of the picture window. All was quiet, save for the birds fighting the remains of the day. I felt sad—that wasn't new—but also as though I'd experienced some sort of reset. With just a few simple words, his friend had planted a seed. Did I need to water it or uproot it? I'd spent these months believing, for the most part, that he was returning to me because he wanted to, but having been reminded of the chaos of our early years, I felt a growing sense of responsibility. I stood there for a long while as my weary mind turned over and over. Eventually I began to ache. Allowing my shoulders to slump, I accepted once again that I had no choice but to carve out a new path or stay here forever.

This time, I knew that a change was coming.

As I stood in the centre of our home, I found myself trying to speak, but my heart fought me, not wanting to hear the words aloud. It was so painful that all parts of me went to war with one another.

"Is it you or is it me?" My stomach turned, and a sickening sensation built in my chest. "Am I supposed to let you go this time?"

The moment the words left me, tears began to fall. After all the back-and-forth and rationalizations over the last four months, I now accepted what I'd likely known all along—I didn't know what was best for him.

I stepped back and gently collided with the shelving unit containing our wineglasses and cocktail glasses. They rattled as I dropped to my knees, my head in my hands. I cried for only a brief time before raising my gaze to the room. I'd been hoping to find him standing before me, his hand reaching out to take mine, assuring me that he wanted us to carry on this dance together. I'd taken for granted the many times he'd reached out that hand to pull us from the mud in which we'd so often found ourselves knee-deep.

He wasn't in front of me, but I could feel him the way I had on my return to the house a short time ago. I gradually stood. Feeling a chill, I wrapped my arms around myself and then glanced out of the window once more before turning and shuffling toward the kitchen. As I moved, I felt a gentle weight against my back. It wasn't heavy—it felt as though it was guiding me. My feet touched the floor, but it was as if I were gliding as I crossed the kitchen. I stopped before the windows overlooking our backyard.

What was left of the sun peered through tree limbs and our wooden fence and cast shadows across the grass. A ray of light was focused directly on the brick patio space adjacent to his pumpkin garden. And that's where I found him again. I startled only slightly and then remained very still. He was seated in one of our chairs with his back to the garden, looking directly at me. He made no attempt to let me know that he could see me, though. He simply stared straight through me, his expression vacant, the sunlight illuminating his pale face.

My heart pounding, I fought every instinct to run to him. Something told me to allow him to determine what would happen next. As I waited, hoping for a signal from him, something moved in the garden behind him. Fallen leaves, I assumed.

Seconds later, I realized that it was something else. It was moving slowly across the ground toward his chair.

Four months ago, I would have shaken my head and found every possible logical explanation for what was happening. Now, however, I watched in a trancelike state as a vine weaved its way from the dirt to his seat. As it approached, another began to make the same journey. These were followed by a third and a fourth vine, all vibrant and strong.

They coiled themselves around the chair, and one wrapped itself around his right ankle before winding up the length of his leg. Another weaved itself around his waist, binding him to the chair, though without any sense of malice. The other vines slid across his arms before working their way over his chest, shoulders, and neck.

He didn't move, but his expression became peaceful. His features softened. It was as though the vines were bringing him comfort. He didn't protest nor struggle as they affectionately navigated their way around his body. He continued to hold my stare, and I got the sense that, like when I saw him on the trail that day in March, he was orchestrating this scene and I was meant to witness it.

As one of the vines moved gently across his face, he turned his head slightly toward the yard, catching the light. A smile formed on his lips, and he tilted his head to the left, allowing the vine to caress his cheekbone. He was swathed in them now, and had it not been for his face and body language, I would have been terrified by the sight. Instead, I found it beautiful and somehow erotic. In fact, something about it felt entirely natural. It was as though I'd seen this image of him before, and its familiarity gave me comfort.

The vines continued to travel about his frame as he stared into the dying sun with a haunting stillness about him. Only in recent months had I ever seen him look so at ease, and each of those times it had been here in our yard, the sun soothing the silent war inside of him. It seemed as though we were mere seconds from being transported back to one of those August afternoons—the afternoons where there'd be no space between us and I could reach out to run my fingers along his thigh.

The longer I watched him, though, the more I sensed that I'd overstayed my welcome. Whatever he'd wanted to say, he'd said it. This was no longer about me. What was happening was now for him and him alone. Still, it was nearly impossible to pull myself away. Something was drawing to a close, and this realization wrecked me.

I forced myself to look away from him, and then, finally, I turned and walked from the room, leaving him to his place in this time. I glanced over my shoulder only once, hoping to see him looking my way or asking me to return, but he remained entranced by the setting sun, his body coiled in the arms of solace.

I moved sullenly to the living room and stood in the centre of the floor once again, unsure of what to do next. My breath caught and my heart raced as I fought the excruciating urge to run to him. I clenched my fists. A hurricane of emotions stormed through my body. I needed him. I needed him to ground me and explain what was happening. Only days ago, I'd agreed to try to move forward and reestablish some semblance of a life. To at least develop a healthy routine. But in a moment, I was thrown back into the violence of existing only for him. Instead of trying to make sense of what, where, and who I was supposed to be now, I was still waiting for him to carry us through this.

I looked back toward the kitchen. He hadn't spoken to me, and he hadn't given me any indication that he needed me. The more I envisioned him there in our yard, the more I realized that he existed somewhere else now, just as I did. We were in this house together, but both trying to make our way through this journey in a space where the other simply couldn't be.

January 2024

FROM OUR BED, I watched him stare out of his window into the night. Occasionally his fingers would play along the ledge, or he'd absentmindedly drag his toes in a circular motion on the hardwood floor. The moon lit his face, chest, and torso, and I found myself aroused. He was lost in whatever space he inhabited while standing here each evening.

I rarely spoke when he was at his window for fear of disturbing him, knowing that he seemed to need this time. It was cold in the room with the window open, though, and I wanted his warmth next me and to feel my limbs intertwined with his. I fell asleep this way most winter nights, laced around him as though our very survival depended on it. There was no greater comfort than his body.

"Baby," I said softly. "I'm cold."

"That's just your heart," he said, without looking at me.

I laughed and pulled the blankets down on his side of the bed. "Come here."

He glanced over his shoulder, then peered out of the window one last time before making his way to the bed. He was about to climb in, and then he looked down at his nightstand. He stared at it for several moments.

"What is it?" I asked.

He reached toward it. When his hand was on the drawer, he seemed to consider something. Then he pulled his hand away. With an expression that suggested he was resigning himself to something, he crawled into bed and immediately attached himself to me. He buried his face in my neck, wrapped his leg around both of mine, and slung his left arm around my chest. He felt so good that an involuntary sound of pleasure escaped me. A wave of relaxation ran through my nervous system.

"There we go," I whispered, pulling him in tight.

I stroked his hair as I listened to his breathing. To my relief, it was slow, which meant he wasn't taking his anxiety to bed with him tonight.

"I love you so much," I said, kissing the top of his head.

He paused before replying. "I love you too. You know that, right?"

"Of course I do," I said, as I squeezed him. "I'm the luckiest man in the world."

Knowing he had something to say, I tried to stave off sleep. This was a nightly struggle. He couldn't sleep until he'd released some of what was on his mind, and I was able to fall asleep instantly.

"I blamed you for a lot of things," he said, resting his head on my chest. "I let you believe that so many things were your fault rather than take responsibility for them." I sensed genuine remorse in his tone.

"What do you mean?" I asked, uncertain as to where this was coming from.

"Every argument we've ever had, every bad decision we've made—until recently I blamed them all on you, like I was help-less. I let you carry that all this time, and it isn't right. It was shitty of me, and it was never fair to you."

"Shh," I said, trying to pull him closer even though there was no room left between us. "Stop that. I don't worry about those things."

"You should," he said. "You should be angry. You've deserved better from me all these years."

"No. I have the best. No one has ever loved me the way you do."

To my dismay, he slowly pulled his body from mine and turned over so his back was to me.

"You punish yourself," he said. "You always have. You could have had someone stable, someone more like you, and your life could have been different. It could have been better."

"Okay, stop this, now," I said sternly, roughly pulling him back to me and wrapping my legs and arms around him. "You're being foolish. Yes, we took too long to truly build our life together, but I belong with you and you belong right here with me. I wouldn't trade any of it. Not one day. We're past this now."

He pulled my hand to his mouth and kissed it gently, not struggling to free himself of my grasp. He inhaled deeply and took his time before he spoke again.

"It isn't your fault that we didn't have kids," he said quietly.

This took the air from me, and I found myself loosening my arms. I released him and rolled onto my back, sighing. "If I were younger—"

"No. At my worst I let you believe that it was your fault we couldn't have kids, and it wasn't. I didn't know I wanted them until it was too late, and my life was a fucking mess—I was a fucking mess. I let you think it was your fault because it made these decisions easier to accept. I don't blame you. If I'd gotten myself together sooner, maybe things would have been different. I cost us everything and you could have had a great life."

He was killing me inside. I never wanted to discuss this, and spent time hoping that he'd one day accept us for who and where we were, and learn to focus on what was to come rather than what could no longer be. No matter what he said, I'd always blame myself and our age gap for the things he now couldn't experience. He rolled over then, placing his back to me and seeming almost ashamed of himself.

"My love," I said. "I live a charmed life with you. The way you take care of us is beautiful, and I'm so thankful for you. I couldn't imagine life without you. Yes, I'll always wonder about these things too, these choices we've made, but what I want more than anything is you." I paused and turned my head to face the back of his. I gently shoved him. "Do you hear me?" I asked. "It's you. It's always been you."

He didn't respond, so I grabbed his shoulder, rolled him over to face me, then used my limbs to draw him close once again. There were tears in his eyes, and this pained me, but I felt desperate to make myself clear.

"I need you to find peace with where we are, with where you are. I love this life with you. Without you, it's nothing. I'm happy. You make me so happy and I wish, I truly wish you knew that and that you could fully accept what we are, and focus on the time we still have together."

His voice broke, and a tear ran down his cheek and onto his pillowcase. "But I've been so awful to you. I want time back. I want all of those years back and I want us to be good to each other and start daydreaming together sooner."

"I know," I said, kissing his cheek and wiping away his tear. "I want that too—very much. But what we have is something truly special and you know that. We're so lucky."

He nodded and extended his neck to kiss me. "I know. I just wish."

I exhaled and he nestled his head back onto my chest. These were wounds that would never be mended, but I believed my words. I believed that our life together was worth the road we'd travelled and that we'd be happy so long as we remained together.

"How's your ankle?" he asked, in a sudden but welcome change of subject. "It's been bothering you lately."

"It's fine," I said, suspicious. There was no way that this conversation had been put to rest. It would return to us time and time again as the years passed. How could it not?

"Are you sure you're okay to run in the morning? I don't want you to feel you have to keep doing this for me if it's hurting you. Maybe it's time for you to slow down."

Hearing this stung, but I knew it hadn't come from a place of cruelty. He was taking care of me. More than once he'd drawn attention to the fact that I was slowing in some ways. I hated this about myself and about us, but I wouldn't let him down. I would never let him down again.

"I'm fine." I kissed his head once more. "Thank you for worrying, but I'm fine. I'll be with you. Hopefully the storm holds off."

He tickled my arm and kissed my chest. "We've run through worse. We can take it." He sniffled, and I felt some of the tension leave his shoulders. "I love you. I love you so much, and I wouldn't want to be anywhere but here with you. Please don't doubt that for a second."

"I'm worried you feel I'm holding you back now," I admitted.

"You saved me," he said. "I've never thanked you for that. For staying." He took my chin in his hand and pulled my face to his. "You saved me from myself by being right here, right now, and there is no life without you in it, no matter what I say. Do you understand? This is hard and it will get harder, but you are everything to me and I'm not going anywhere. But we have to promise each other there will be no more regrets. No more should-haves. Okay?" He kissed me and then locked his gaze with mine. "And you're not going anywhere either. I fucking dare you to try."

I smiled and squeezed him as tightly as I could, overcome with relief and happiness even though I didn't fully believe he'd never go. His realism over the years had changed me, and doubt sometimes existed where before it hadn't.

"I love you," I told him again. "Please try to get some sleep, okay? We'll have a great run tomorrow."

I released my hold only enough for him to get reasonably comfortable. Minutes later I fell asleep to the sound of his breathing and the feel of his skin warming the deepest corners of my insides. I awoke only once in the night to the sensation of his finger running gently up and down my spine. I fell back to sleep almost immediately under his watchful eye.

A few hours later, the alarm sounded. I kissed him softly and held him for a moment before pulling myself from the bed. As I stepped around it on my way to the bathroom, he reached up and grabbed my arm. I stopped and looked down at him on the bed.

"Hey," he whispered. "You and me."

I leaned down to kiss him again. "You and me," I whispered back.

Silently, we got ourselves dressed and made our way downstairs to prepare for our run.

May 2024

IT TOOK ME two more weeks' worth of brutal conversations with myself, but I managed to recommence the process of packing away our life together into boxes, which now rested in small stacks throughout the house. I'd tried to be ruthless when deciding what to keep, donate, or throw away, but I wasn't the man I'd been years ago. I'd once attached little sentimental value to belongings—now I struggled with the idea of parting with something that might hold even a single memory of him or us. I'd find myself placing an item in the *throw away* pile only to later feel a sense of panic and pull it from its miserable fate. Still, I managed.

As the days passed, it became easier. I was going to bed at reasonable hours, drinking even less wine, and using what willpower I could muster not to ask for him. He crossed my mind every hour and with every piece of clothing or cutlery I touched, but I forced myself not to wish for him to come to me. More than once, though, I was reduced to tears, wishing that this process was being undertaken because we were leaving together, a new adventure on the horizon. Doing this without him and committing to the decisions I'd made on my own just made him feel all the more gone. It hurt me in ways I'd believed I was now beyond.

He returned to me only once during this time, on his own. I'd been lying in bed, holding the engagement ring that he'd never place on my finger, and allowing the tears to flow freely. I was repeating the words he'd written—and likely rehearsed for his proposal—over and over out loud. Each time, I strained to hear them in his voice rather than my own. When I began to collapse in on myself, clutching the ring to my chest, that's when he came.

He appeared at his window but spent no time gazing out of it. With his eyes on me, he crossed the room and climbed into the bed beside me. He lay on his back and then turned his body to face mine. His smiled, and there was a sad but understanding shimmer in his eyes. We stared into each other until my tears dried and my breathing became more regulated. He remained there with me long enough for me to fall asleep. When I woke, he was gone.

I'd promised us both that I'd try to do this without him, so I put the ring away and told myself that for the time being, I wasn't allowed to hold it. I was incapable of doing so without feeling crushed under the weight of regret and all the things that might have been. With that would inevitably come the temptation to ask him to come to me and let me know that it was okay, that it would be okay. It wouldn't, and I knew that. I needed to find my way forward despite this.

As difficult as sorting through the house was, dealing with the logistics of our shop was almost worse. I'd worked with a lawyer in recent weeks and placed the bulk of the responsibility on his family to navigate the sale. There was no way I could continue there without him, and it would do neither of us any good for me to try. Our dream was over now, and I needed it gone.

I'd returned today only to gather the belongings that wouldn't be included in the sale and to ensure I hadn't left anything of his behind. I also wanted to clean the front steps of the shop. After his passing, many people had left flowers on these steps. I'd ignored them that night I visited, and likely because no one knew the protocol for removing dead bouquets from a tribute, they'd remained there on the steps, an apocalyptic scene adjacent to the sidewalk. I felt compelled to clear them away now and save others the dilemma. I'd ignored their attempts to show care or to help. I could at least show them the courtesy and respect of sweeping away the debris before I left this place behind.

I entered from the back of the shop and walked its length to the front door, hoping to avoid all contact. I still couldn't muster the strength to have a meaningful dialogue with anyone, especially those who only claimed to have known him. I couldn't and wouldn't meet them at that level for the sake of keeping up appearances. I opened the door cautiously and peered through before fully emerging—and startled when I found someone waiting outside of it. It took me a moment to realize who they were, and when I did, I was as irritated as I was confused by this person's presence.

"Hi there," they said carefully. "Sorry I scared you."

I shook my head. "No, it's fine. You know we've been closed for months."

They smiled. "Of course I knew. I just wondered if I might find you here, and here you are."

"How could you possibly have known I was going to be here?" I asked angrily.

They shrugged and smiled. "Okay, I saw your car pull around back. I happened to be passing by."

I tried to refrain from rolling my eyes, but once again they left the station without me. Fortunately, they seemed to be a person of thick skin, one who understood human emotion and wasn't going to hold this against me. Being who I now was, I offered no apology.

"I won't force you to talk to me," they said. "And I definitely don't mean to intrude. But I thought that I might be able to help you in some way if you'll just give me a second."

I exhaled loudly and leaned against the door. I had two choices: let them in and endure what came next, or stand here with the door open, inviting any passersby to take notice and undoubtedly stop. I chose the lesser of two evils and unenthusiastically ushered them in.

"Grab a seat," I grumbled, locking the door behind them. "I'll be with you in a minute."

"Sure," they said, removing their bag from their shoulder and placing it on one of the tables.

"Not so close to the window. I don't need people—"

"Seeing you here. Of course, yes." They obliged and moved two more tables inward.

I made my way behind the bar and quickly sifted through drawers of papers in a filing cabinet. He'd hired this person several times to perform tarot readings at the shop, but not once had I asked for their name, not caring what it was. It was possible he had some sort of agreement that referenced them tucked away somewhere, and I furiously removed everything from the filing cabinet in a desperate attempt to find it. I had struggled with pronouns, not out of ignorance, but as a queer man from an earlier generation. I had learning to do. Not wanting to get it wrong, I scrambled to find anything that would save me the embarrassment. After a minute or two, though, it occurred to me that I still didn't care. Why was I letting this bother me? They had invited themself here, I didn't know them, and I had no time for them. Annoyed with myself, I left the bar area with the intention of getting them out of the shop as soon as possible.

He'd liked this person. They'd connected somehow. He hadn't outright believed in what they'd had to say, but there was something about their personalities and perspectives that was similar, and I'd enjoyed how easily their conversation had flowed. He'd never pushed me to allow this person to read me, as he knew my stance on this was firm. Over the years he'd eased up on trying to instill these beliefs in me, about the unexplainable, but he still held out hope that I'd make room for the possibilities. Over these last few months, he'd won that fight. And in doing so, he'd left me a shattered man full of questions, fear, hope, and devastation. His love had always done the same, though, and I was a better person for it.

As I approached the table, I saw they were laying out their tarot cards. Rage boiled underneath my skin.

"No," I said sternly. "No, no, no."

They held up their hands and spoke gently. "I will not, I promise you, tell you anything that I think might hurt you. I came here to do exactly the opposite—"

"I said fucking no," I snapped. "Who the hell do you think you are, showing up here and laying your bullshit out in front of me this way? I have no time for this. None. What the fuck were you even doing skulking around outside?"

I could see them tense. They placed their hands on the table but kept their eyes on me. They were kind, and the sympathy they'd offered me shortly after he passed had felt different from others' condolences. There was also an edge to them. I recalled how matter-of-fact they'd been. They'd spoken to him with a refreshing directness.

I relaxed only slightly, not prepared to relent but wanting to, again, at least try to be someone who could find the good in people. I wanted to keep the best parts of him inside of me, and that meant being open and it meant being kind.

"I'm sorry," I said quietly. "I've been very isolated these past months and have had almost no interest in conversation." I looked down at them, this well-meaning person whom he might have considered a friend. "I don't believe in what you do. I know he believed in these things sometimes, but I never did and I take no comfort in it. I appreciate you coming by, but it's best if you just go."

They nodded and began to carefully retract their cards. They seemed childlike as they went about the task, as though they'd been asked to put away their toys.

"I lost someone," they said. "Two years ago. I lost someone very important to me and there was not one goddamn thing anyone could say or do to help."

They glanced up at me. I didn't interrupt them. They were leaving anyway. They could talk their way out.

"I remember the phone calls, the uninvited visitors. All the flowers and emails and texts. Every single one made me fucking angrier than the last. Like any of those people had any idea, right?"

I crossed my arms over my chest, conceding that I felt the pain in their words. "Right," I said. "He always told me I was great with people but that I could be a real asshole when I wanted to be. I'd say I've outdone myself lately."

They smiled and nodded. "My own mother doesn't call me anymore. One day she caught me at just the absolute worst time and without even meaning to, I called her a meddling cunt."

I afforded them a small grin and nodded. "I had a similar phone exchange with a do-gooder a while back. I meant no harm but made no attempt to fix it either."

Their belongings were back in their bag, and they graciously wiped the table with their sleeve. Before they rose, they opened their palms on the table and looked at me with an expression of both fear and determination.

"He isn't suffering," they said. "I think it's important that you know that. He's not in any pain."

I wanted to scream. I wanted to grab them by their arm and throw them through the door before they could utter one more word. At the same time, tears filled my eyes and a familiar ache returned to my heart. My hands shook.

"Don't," I said, my voice cracking. "Just shut up."

"I will. But if you'll let me, I think I can offer you some answers. You don't have to believe in what I do to hear them." They paused, and I struggled not to sob. "He is okay, but there are things he's going to need from you. You can choose not to hear me, but if you don't, you might remain stuck in whatever it is I think you're going through for the rest of your life."

I let my arms drop to my sides. My chest heaved. "Please stop," I said, my eyes closed and voice firm. I pointed at the door, but my arm felt too heavy to raise more than a few inches. "Stop."

"And he's going to be stuck in it with you."

I suddenly felt the need to defend myself, to tell them that I knew this and that I was working harder to help him find peace. This would have been for my own benefit, though. It had nothing to do with them. I took a deep breath, opened my eyes, and took them in. I could no longer decide if I wanted them gone or if I wanted to pull from them everything I could.

The very idea that they could know anything of where he was, what he was feeling, or what was happening made me drunk with desperation. I hadn't recognized myself over the last four months, but one thing that had remained was my ability to put up a wall when confronted with anything I didn't have the mental capacity to deal with. I was defenceless against what was happening between him and me, but to anyone on the outside I was cold. This exchange, however, had left me feeling something else. As I considered them, I thought about him and his willingness to try. He would try and he would learn, and he would always allow himself to believe in the very ideas that I'd often block.

I could try for him now, I thought. I could listen and I could try for him, and maybe there'd be something in this that could help him, if not me. If he was as stuck as I was and someone could help him find his way through, I owed it to him to talk to this person.

I pulled out a chair across from them at the table. Sitting down, I looked at them with disdain so as to make it clear I wasn't succumbing to what I still believed to be make-believe. I placed my hands on the table and clasped them. "If you say one thing that disrespects him or makes light of us, I'll shut this down," I said, with only enough severity to make my point.

"I told you I didn't come here to hurt you. I won't hurt him, either. You can stop me at any time."

I nodded slowly. There was a storm in my gut, and I was unsure whether I could speak the words I wanted to. My thumbs danced as I contemplated how far I could go. Finally, I decided this would be a conversation I'd have once, and one time only. If I was going to open myself to this, I might as well do so fully and walk away knowing I'd tried. Plus, I'd never encounter this person again: This I knew.

"I see him," I said quietly.

They didn't speak. Instead, they waited for me to find myself and the courage I needed.

"Not ... it isn't a vision," I continued. "I see him, and it's really him. I've touched him."

Adrenaline followed by a sense of release coursed through me. I'd spoken the words out loud. All these months I'd existed with him, in our space. I'd been so deep inside of it, and this was the first time I'd yanked myself out. Even as I felt a weight leave me, I also felt a heavy sadness, a renewed sense of loss. What was happening was ours and it was us, and I'd now let someone else in.

"Okay," they said, in a soft, cautious tone. "You're asleep when you see him? Or you see him when you're awake?"

"Awake," I admitted, my voice timid. "Both, but awake. A few times."

"Okay. I'm going to ask you some questions. Is that all right?"

"Fuck no," I said, exhaling. "But go ahead."

They smiled sympathetically. "Does he seem angry when you see him?"

I thought back to our encounters: the first evening in our bedroom, the night in the living room, the day on the trail, the evening at the shop, the night when he lay next to me in bed, the time he appeared in our yard. Then I recalled the night that our former friend stopped by.

"Only once," I said. "Usually he watches me and takes care of me. Only once was he angry. There was someone else in the house with me and ... he was there. I wasn't afraid because I understood. He'd have reacted the same way to the situation had he been alive, so it just felt like he was really there." My head spun. I was talking too much. "I think I'm going to be sick."

They narrowed their eyes and seemed determined to push forward. "Does he seem sad?"

I gathered myself as best as I could and thought about it. This question was more complicated. "I'm sad when he comes. Actually, I seem to be at my worst when he comes. A couple of times he seemed as sad as I was, and one time he was … in the state he'd died in …"

I was going much too far. This wasn't me, and recounting these details was making the floor spin. I needed to stop. This wasn't helping.

"I know, obviously, what happened. It was local news." They patted my hand in a manner that would have been condescending had almost anyone else done it. "And I'm sorry for that. I wish that hadn't been his passage, both for his sake and yours."

"Are you going to say something helpful at some point? Because I really do think I might vomit." I placed a hand on my chest.

"When someone dies a violent death, the chaos of that can hold them in time."

They paused, perhaps waiting for me to silence them, but I was too nauseated to protest. Also, this was what I'd wanted. Even if I learned nothing here, he might, so I'd see this through.

"He's quite possibly stuck amongst the fear and pain of that event," they said. "If so, he'll have a hard time moving forward."

I looked up, angry. "You told me he isn't suffering."

"He isn't. He's not feeling pain, but I believe he's feeling trapped in a place that's surrounded by chaos."

"I can't stop it from having happened. How am I supposed to help him deal with something that can't be undone?"

They hesitated, and I braced myself, fearing the breaking point was imminent and I'd momentarily be escorting them out in a headlock.

"If you'll allow me this …"

"Go ahead, but get to whatever the point is, fast," I said, glaring at them.

"He's coming to you when you're at your worst. I'm going to assume that you speak his name or call out to him in some way during these times. You make it clear that you need him and are unable to move forward from the place you're in without him. This is what's keeping him here. This, along with the details of his death and the fact that he was taken from you before he felt he'd lived his life with you."

We stared at each other for a moment.

"You're both hanging on to each other," they said softly. "You're loving each other in a way that's maintaining the tie between you that …"

"That what?" I asked, a lump forming in my throat.

"That needs to be severed," they said, looking as though they were feeling genuine pain for me. "For now. I don't know your relationship and I only spoke to him a few times, but anyone could see the way that you loved each other. There was an energy between you that was more force than emotion. We should all be so lucky to have that in our lives, and I'm sorry that it has to change. You don't want my opinion, so that isn't what I'm giving you. What I can speak from is experience, and believe me or don't, but you're hurting each other by refusing to allow the other to move forward. He may not be suffering, but he is stuck, and he won't be happy where he is—and maybe neither will you?"

I was drained, completely empty. With no fight left and nothing more to give, I turned my head and gazed out of the window toward Main Street. I felt ill. I needed a hot bath and a bed but didn't have the energy to find my way home, and wondered how I would.

"I try," I said, not to them but to the space around us. "I try, but he's in everything. He's in me, and if he wasn't, I'm not sure I'd survive."

They took a deep breath and regarded me the way a patient teacher would a challenging student. "You have your beliefs, and you choose your own path. Just know that your choices are helping to shape his path as well."

With that, they stood and made their way to the door. I was glad to see them go but thanked them for their time and for hearing me out. I regretted having shared so much of myself, but more than that, I felt ashamed. This was the second time that someone had made clear to me that I was largely responsible for what was happening between us—that if I let go or at least tried to, perhaps he'd be better off.

Seeing him dragged and torn to his death was an agony from which I'd never recover. Being unable to share with him every detail of our life was gutting. The understanding that I'd finally have to let go of him was a hurt so indescribable that it took me back to the moment I looked down at his bloodstained face and realized he was gone.

The idea that I could be causing him further harm was worse than any pain I'd experienced thus far.

I looked around our shop, the place we'd built together on nothing but a dream and our belief that together, we could do anything. My heart was heavy as I gathered the items I'd come for, looked around one last time, and then left it behind, uttering a quiet goodbye.

June 2024

BIRDS SANG, THE sun shone, and I felt the breeze that would have tousled his sandy hair as he dreamily stared off into his gardens on an afternoon just like this. I allowed this image of him to warm me, to hurt me momentarily, and then I set it aside. I opened the rickety door of our shed and peeked inside to ensure I hadn't left behind anything of value. It was empty save for the tools that the new owners were gladly taking off my hands. I was happy to leave behind anything they'd shown interest in. As much as I'd struggled to let go of material possessions recently, I knew that what mattered and what was worth fighting to keep were the memories, the sensations, the words, and the impacts that both people and experiences left you holding once they were gone.

Satisfied that I could place a final check mark on the shed, I closed the door and walked away from it without turning back. I didn't think about him dragging the lawn mower from it, having a cocktail, and then setting out to cut the grass, headphones on. I didn't think about the Christmas lights we'd strung along its tin roof each December. I simply left it and summoned the willpower to do so without guilt. He wasn't inside this shed any more than he was inside any room within the house itself. He was gone from here now, and that was okay.

I walked the brick path back to the house and stepped inside, repeating to myself over and over out loud that this was no longer our house and that I wasn't leaving him here. I walked the rooms of the main level. All signs of our existence had been donated or taken to the dump. I had enlisted the help of a couple of local friends I'd reengaged with. Had I been able to get through the logistics of this process alone, I would have, but these people had the equipment and the resources to make things happen. Their willingness to forgive my behaviour and help me get out of this house had been a godsend, and I'd tried to show my genuine appreciation. They were good people, and they deserved better than the way I'd treated them.

I paused in the living room and stood before the picture window to look out at the front yard and the afternoon traffic on the street beyond. Summer had arrived, and it could be felt in the energy of those going about their day-to-day. Steps were lighter, and a sense of ease had settled over the town. I had managed to set myself on a new course, and had made myself many new promises, but days like this hurt. I'd endeavoured to be gone before June, but everything had taken time and now here I was. I did my best not to imagine him going from room to room to open windows, or standing out back excitedly making plans for the vegetables he had no idea how to grow. Our couch was gone and for that I was glad—had it been here now, I might have succumbed and lain upon it to imagine him next to me awaiting an impending summer storm.

I gave myself a small shake and turned away from the window. As I did, I had a flashback to the night he stood behind me here, wrapping my body in his. I felt the memory in my stomach and left the room in an attempt to leave it where it had happened, though I knew it would never be that easy. These hadn't been visions and they hadn't been dreams. He'd been here, and this truth would live within me and change the way I viewed almost everything. I could file these flashbacks only to the best of my ability—old me and new me would have to fight that fight. Coping and moving forward were currently the only expectations I'd placed on myself.

I opened the door to the basement and made my way down the stairs. The farewell to this room proved to be the most difficult. The evenings down here, both with him and on my own, were the times I'd felt the most at home in this house. The comfort he'd established in this space had endured through my cold, wine-soaked nights. I'd donated the movies and albums his friends and family hadn't wanted, and had allowed myself to keep a small selection in the end. The donations had all been packed and taped, but then a song would come to mind, and I'd recognize it as something he'd introduced me to. The sense of panic would return, and I'd tear into the boxes to retrieve the CD it was on and add it to the small number of items I was keeping. I allowed myself to make these reconsiderations only a handful of times before cutting myself off, knowing I was on a slippery slope.

The room was empty now, but not emptier than it had felt since he left. I'd spent those early months trying to relive every night here with him, and that had kept him close. Now I was able to take one last look around and remind myself that though we had shared this space, it was no longer ours. Our workouts as he chattered at me incessantly, the nights in front of the television—they'd live inside of me, but they didn't live here.

I made the necessary phone calls to finalize the details of my move the following morning. I opened and closed every cupboard for the third time to be certain no small artifact had been left behind. I ate my leftover takeout from the night before, threw the container into a garbage bag I'd opened for this purpose, and then walked the bag out to the curb. The sky was darkening, and I looked at the house from the end of the driveway, taking it in under the twilight. I could see his maple tree in the back yard, rustling in a soft breeze. I stopped myself just before picturing him under it, lying on his back and staring up through the leaves. He'd taught me to thank things before leaving them behind. He'd stopped me to do this the morning we left our condo in the city. He'd done it in hotel rooms and parks. He'd thanked entire countries while boarding a plane. Everything he did left a mark on him, and he felt compelled to acknowledge it. It wasn't any wonder he never slept. I smiled a melancholy smile, quietly thanked the large maple, and made my way back inside for my final night in our home.

I brushed my teeth, flossed, took one last look at my phone, and then double-checked my suitcase. Everything was meticulously folded, right down to my underwear. He'd once told me I packed like a serial killer. The memory made me smile. The differences between us had held firm right to the end, and I was happy about that. Had it not been for the things that separated us, we would never have learned as much as we had. I was thankful for every single time he'd cocked his head and given me a look of total perplexity. I was equally grateful for every time he'd left me with clenched fists in a state of utter bewilderment.

Admitting that there was nothing left to do, no list to run a final check on, I turned off the hallway light and headed to our bedroom. In the centre of the floor was the air mattress on which we'd spent our first sleepless night in this house, as well as the photo of us in the city, which I had reframed. It rested on its stand beside the head of the mattress with the image turned to face my pillow. I could have slept in any other room this final night. I could have booked a hotel on the road or stayed with friends. Instead, I'd decided to have one last night in our bedroom to say goodbye to the beautiful four years we'd shared here. I wanted him to know how much of a loss this was, and that I wasn't leaving it behind easily—as though he hadn't proven that he was seeing every step and every tear this process had required.

Staring at the mattress, I felt myself sink slightly. Perhaps this was too much, this recreation of our first night. Perhaps I was asking too much of myself. A sickening sensation I hadn't felt in several weeks began to settle on my chest, but rather than surrender to it, I rolled my shoulders a couple of times and looked toward his window. I hesitated for only a few seconds before taking the three steps to it. I placed my fingers on the ledge and leaned forward to look at our backyard. The summer moon stared down at me, and I smiled back up at it. I even allowed myself a moment to remember his face as he would talk about the stars and who or what may be hiding amongst them. I'd made this my nightly ritual as of late, a compromise with myself. I'd do my best to move on without him, but I'd allow myself to reestablish connections with what had been meaningful to him. I could do what I needed to do to feel close to him without asking for him. I could do that.

The window was open wide, and through it came the familiar summer smells of grass and farmlands. I inhaled them and welcomed the sounds of crickets and the occasional bullfrog. It didn't matter the season—he'd stood here just like this night after night. I still couldn't put my finger on what had held his attention and seemingly his heart. Standing here, however, did make me feel calm, and I hoped he'd felt the same. It was ours, this yard, this house, the summer nights in the grass. It was our piece of life, and we had existed here together. It was a space that no one else would ever encroach upon. They couldn't.

I turned from the window, feeling as though he were inside of me, and followed what I felt were his steps to the mattress, positioned precisely where our bed once was. I pulled down the one sheet I'd left unpacked and slid under it. Turning onto my right side, I looked at the photograph. A sense of unease returned to my stomach, but before it could take root, I kissed my index finger and reached over to touch his face in the picture.

"Good night, babe," I said, and then rolled to my left side and to my own surprise, began to drift into sleep.

Hours later I lay awake crying, and debated getting up to begin my journey rather than see the night through. It had been a mistake believing I could do this or that it would be good for either of us. I'd already forgotten his advice to leave when it was time. I should have left when I felt strong, but I'd convinced myself that I owed us this night.

I wiped my eyes and took a deep breath, trying with every fibre of my being not to wish for him. How was this possible? How was it possible that I'd live a life without him when my heart would forever remain trapped in the thirteen years we'd had together? Trying to move on when I had no desire to was a war that I'd wage within myself every day for the remainder of this life. I had no doubt about that. I'd never find peace without him. The sickening sensation returned to my chest.

I forced myself to recount a positive memory of him and shake off the self-pity. I remembered his laugh. I remembered our more trivial arguments, during which I'd struggle not to smile at how unreasonably passionate he could be. I remembered his cutting humour and how many times others had fallen silent after a remark he'd made; meanwhile, I'd stifle a laugh. He was joy. He had brought me joy. This was what I'd remember about him always.

Giving up on the idea of sleep, I pulled myself from the mattress and looked around. I'd pack up the few items in this room and I'd make my way. No sooner had I picked up my pillow than another wave of sadness crashed over me and tears sent me back to the mattress. I allowed myself to sob for several minutes. I didn't chastise myself, nor did I allow myself to fall too far. Once I felt sufficiently drained of almost all feeling, I told myself to get up and to gather the remaining material pieces of our life here. Afterward, I walked to his window to take one last look outside.

There he lay, directly beneath the window, in the grassy space just next to his pumpkin patch. His eyes were open, and he was staring at the star-filled sky, one leg crossed over the other, his hands resting on his chest. A light breeze moved through the yard and blew a strand of hair onto his forehead. My instinct was to run to him, climb on top of him, and brush it from his brow, but I remained where I stood. He didn't acknowledge me. A smile slowly formed on his pale, moonlit face. He was the picture of serenity, and I'd never seen him more beautiful.

"Okay," I whispered to myself. "Okay."

Dawn was closer than I'd realized. The sun was beginning to rise as I shoved the box containing the air mattress into the trunk of our SUV. Birds sang, but there were no other signs of life. It would be another hour at least before the world began to turn again. I closed the trunk and stood looking at our home and the neighbourhood that surrounded it. Time healed most things. I knew that. I would never be healed, but perhaps in time I wouldn't miss this place. Perhaps I'd fully embrace the fact that he was inside of me. I didn't need to see him to know that. He'd been part of me before I'd even known him, and he'd remain that way until the day I died. Until the day I could be where he now was. I would find him again, and I knew, with absolute certainty, that we'd pick up our journey right where we'd left off.

"There's nowhere you could go that I wouldn't find you," I said aloud, quoting him.

I smiled, took one last look around, and climbed into the SUV. As I adjusted the rearview mirror, I caught sight of someone moving toward the vehicle from the end of the driveway. He was running toward me with a look of panic, and for a moment I wondered if I was dreaming, though I knew I wasn't. I didn't feel fear as he approached. This wasn't the way he'd run to me when I attempted to revisit the space in the woods. This time, he was running toward me, rather than running to drive me away. My heart raced and my body stiffened. An anxiety I'd never known filled me as I waited for him to reach me. Seconds later, he pulled open the passenger door and climbed inside. He wasn't breathless. He was silent as he sat next to me, staring directly ahead out of the windshield. I was paralyzed but filled with adrenaline.

What had I been thinking? What the hell had either of us been thinking?

He turned to look at me, his expression both devious and hopeful. I stared back at him and felt a smile form. We held each other's gazes for several moments before I started the engine. This wasn't right. I knew that, and he knew that too. But love burned through me like fire. Just as he had in our earliest days, he ran through me like a train and shattered me to pieces. I reached out and ran the back of my index finger along his cheek. He grinned.

"Fuck it," I said. "You and me."

I kicked the car into gear and hit the gas. The tires screeched as we sped away from our house. I made no attempt to make sense of what this was or what it meant for the road ahead. I didn't know where we'd end up, and it didn't matter. I surrendered to myself, to him, to the possibilities, and it felt like home.

Home was anywhere he was.

Acknowledgements

First and foremost, I need to thank my husband. You took many hits to help make this happen, and you are still cheering me on every single step of the way. I've never deserved you.

I also want to thank Ann Campbell, my grade 10 Math and English teacher. Life brought me back home again, and now I get to call you my friend and to make you your Earl Grey. You were the very first person to read this manuscript in its early stages, and you told me to keep going.

A thank you to my mother, who would have thrown every last resource she could have at me to make this happen. You've been telling me to write for years; I hope I make you proud of me.

Thank you to Mike and Virginia for each taking the time on a dark February evening to enlighten me and to help better shape this journey. Thank you to the family and friends who are rooting for me. Sarah, Fin, Erika, Trevor, Lori ... I don't deserve you either.

A huge thanks to the team at Ingenium. Never once did you give me reason to believe the worst voices in my head. You treated me like I have every right to be here, and the lessons I've learned from you have been invaluable.

And finally, I want to thank every boy who ever broke my heart and called me crazy. Ultimately, you fuelled that crazy, and it spun me right into the wide-open arms of the love of my life, who has never wanted me to change a thing. That same crazy drove this story, and will drive many more to come. Still have love for you all—can't help it.

About the Author

A forty-something daydreamer who grew up in Kemptville, Ontario, then lived in Kingston, Ottawa, and Toronto, Scott Godwin now co-owns the award-winning Bubba & Bugs Coffee Bar in his hometown. He worked in the arts for many years before deciding it was time to finally sink his teeth into writing.

Scott lives in Kemptville with his husband and business partner, Luc. Any downtime he has is spent writing, reading, and hiding out in the backyard with the couple's two dogs, Moose and Sweet Pea.

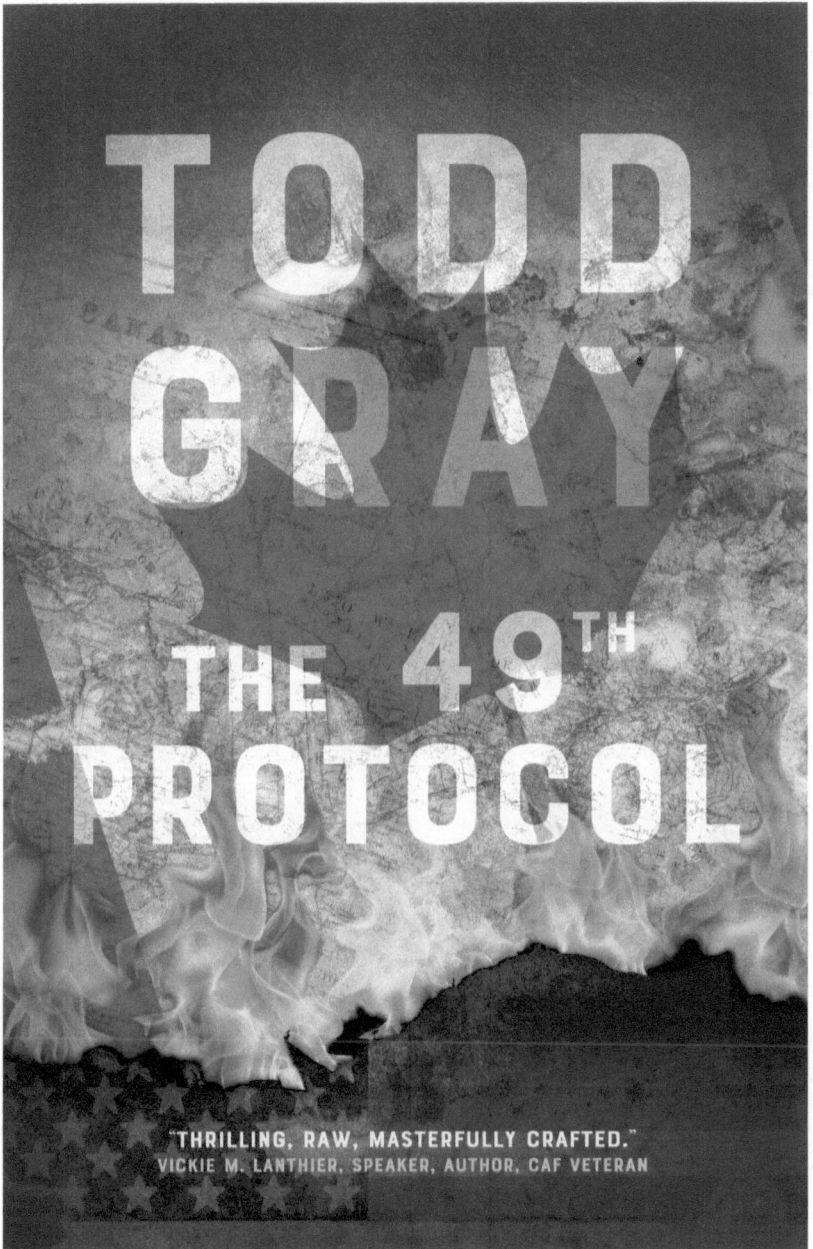

You Might Also Enjoy ...

TODD GRAY

THE 49TH PROTOCOL

"THRILLING, RAW, MASTERFULLY CRAFTED."
VICKIE M. LANTHIER, SPEAKER, AUTHOR, CAF VETERAN

ingeniumbooks.com/49P

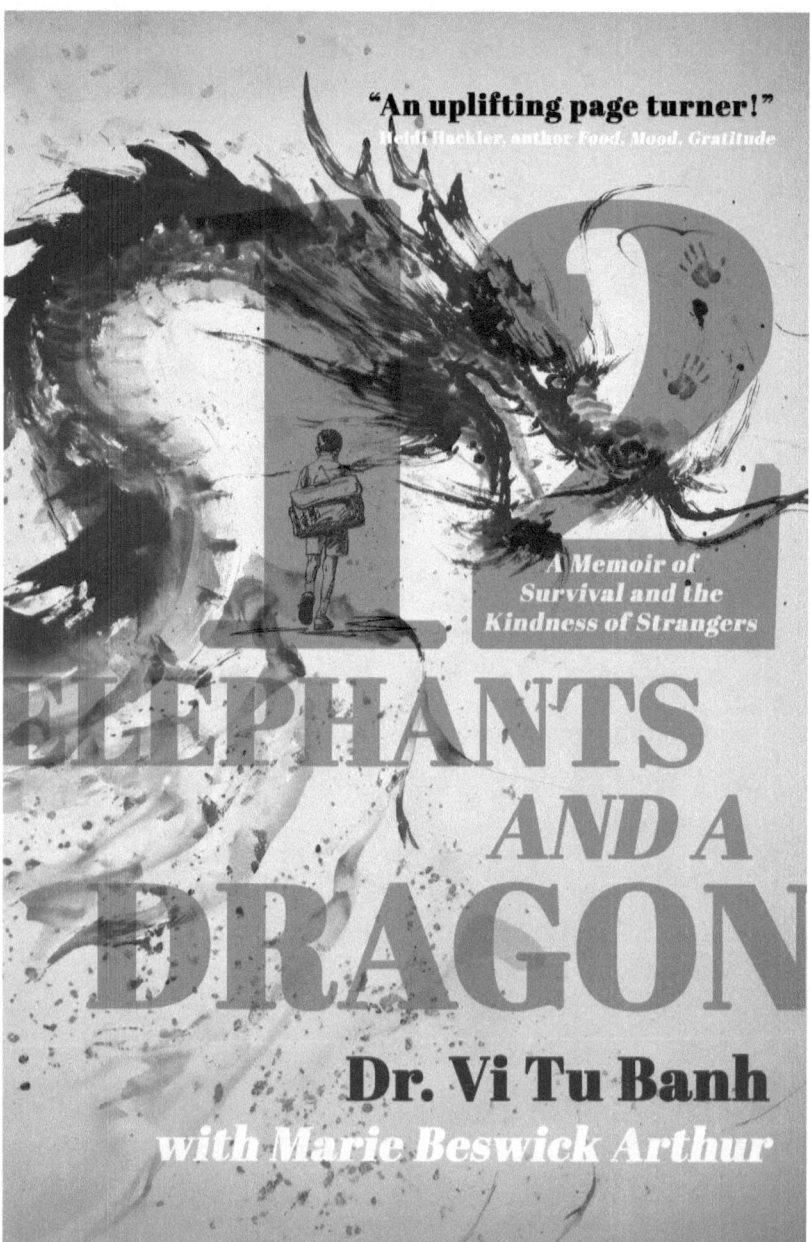

"An uplifting page turner!"
Heidi Hackler, author *Food, Mood, Gratitude*

12

*A Memoir of
Survival and the
Kindness of Strangers*

ELEPHANTS
AND A
DRAGON

Dr. Vi Tu Banh
with Marie Beswick Arthur

ingeniumbooks.com/12ED

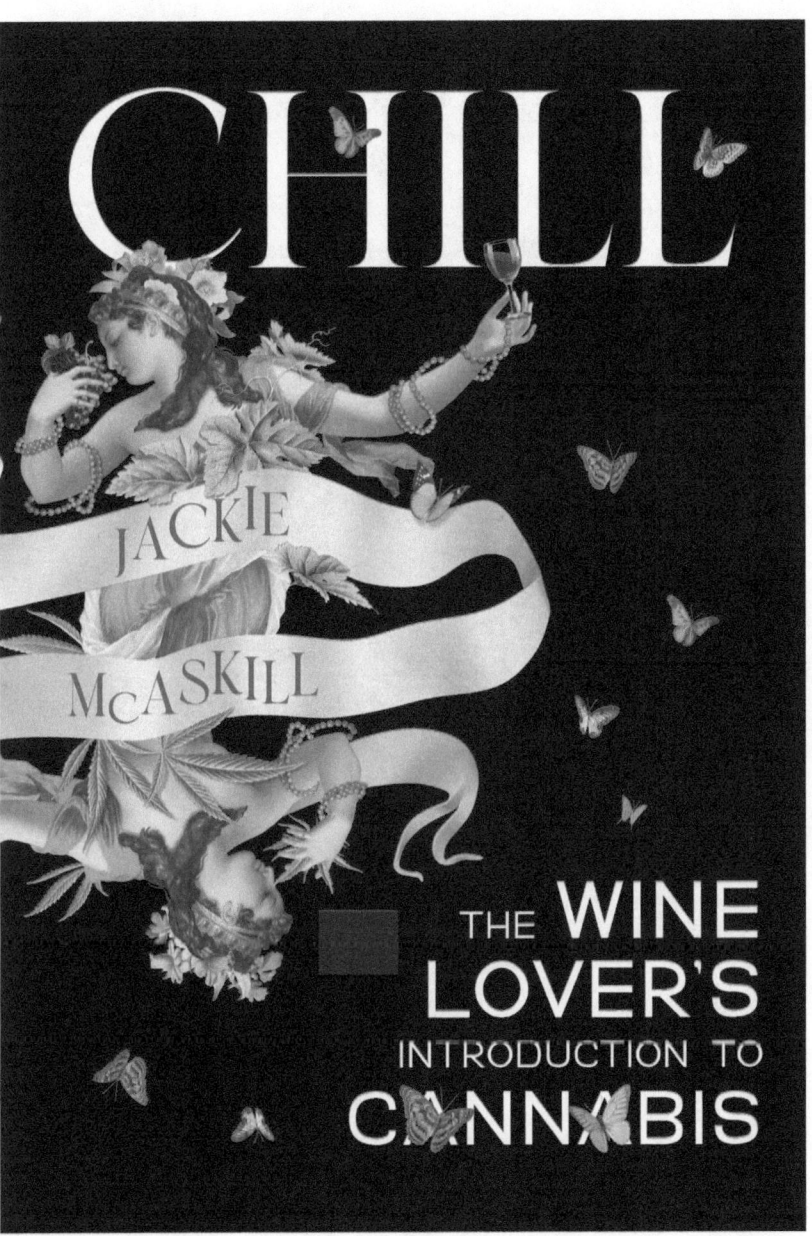

CHILL

JACKIE
McASKILL

THE WINE
LOVER'S
INTRODUCTION TO
CANNABIS

ingeniumbooks.com/CHILL

"UNFORGETTABLE PROSE, MASTERFULLY COMPOSED."
CORA TAYLOR, AWARD-WINNING AUTHOR OF *JULIE* AND *SUMMER OF THE MAD MONK*

LITERARY TITAN
★★★★★
BOOK
AWARD

MARIE BESWICK ARTHUR

LISTEN FOR WATER

ingeniumbooks.com/lfwp

THE WALL STREET JOURNAL BEST SELLER

"TRULY VISIONARY,
INSIGHTFUL, AND RELATABLE.
A BRILLIANT MUST-READ!"
ROBERT ROGERS, PSILOCYBIN MUSHROOMS:
THE MYSTERY, SCIENCE AND RESEARCH

THE **PROMISE** OF **PSYCHEDELICS**

DR. PETER SILVERSTONE

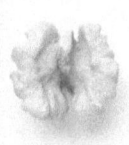 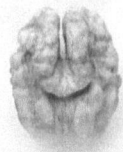  

*Science-Based Hope
for Better Mental Health*

ingeniumbooks.com/0ugf

LAUREN S. CLUCAS

CH♥ICES

HOW TO MEND OR END
A BROKEN RELATIONSHIP

"POIGNANT, POWERFUL, PRACTICAL!"
Verity Price, author *Present with Power*

ingeniumbooks.com/CHCS

"EMPOWERING AND PRACTICAL."
THE HONOURABLE CHANTAL PETITCLERC,
PARALYMPIAN, SENATOR, AND MOTHER

MARJORIE
AUNOS, PHD

PENCRAFT AWARDS
A BEST BOOK
WINNER
SPRING 2023
LITERARY EXCELLENCE

MOM
ON
WHEELS

THE POWER OF PURPOSE FOR
A PARENT WITH PARAPLEGIA

ingeniumbooks.com/as3o